## Praise for Spirit X

"To say Nikola Anandamali Ristic is holistic is like saying the ocean is salty. In Spirit X he casts a remarkably wide net, drawing wisdom from all corners of the vast spiritual terrain, reconciling all kinds of paradoxes, and harmonizing elements that appear to be contradictory but are, from the right perspective and in the right hands, perfectly compatible: the ancient and the ultra-modern; tradition and innovation; inner and outer; spirit and matter; transcendence and immanence; the sacred and the (seemingly) profane; body and soul; visible and invisible; lofty ideas and gritty reality. Above all, the book is as practical as it is inspiring and enjoyable. Readers will find the book a great companion as they move ahead on the spiritual path."

—Philip Goldberg
author of *Spiritual Practice for Crazy Times*,
*The Life of Yogananda* and *American Veda*

"A poetic Integral guide and workbook for the 21st century that skillfully leads us to the unspeakable. Laced with instructions for profound practices, it teaches us how to use every aspect of our life, including love relationships, for waking-up and growing-up to put our gifts and purpose in service of creating a better world. Spirit X should be on every nightstand and coffee table for our daily inspiration and spiritual practice."

—Martin Ucik
author of *Integral Relationships: A Manual for Men* and
*Sex, Purpose, Love: Couples in Integral
Relationships Creating a Better World*

"I loved reading this book. I kept finding myself in it—and then being welcomed to lovingly see others who are different from me. I kept thinking, "I wish everyone saw things this way." Deep, authentic integral wisdom flows from these pages in fresh, understandable ways. It is a practical, inclusive, and beautiful portrait of the many dimensions of spirituality in today's world. I was invited to see meditation and traditional wisdom, along with technology, culture, pop-culture, work, money, and sex as a means of spiritual growth and unfolding. I was given a gracious and breathtaking tour of the world's spiritual traditions, from Shiva to Jesus, dance to bhakti yoga, and transcendence to deity worship. As an intrepid researcher in spirituality, I was surprised at how much I learned from Ristic's elegant insights. I found myself highlighting over 20% of the text! This is for all who are interested in expanding the breadth and depth of their spirituality. I would love to see a significant part of the world's population who are ready for it, read this book."

—Paul Smith
co-founder of the Integral Christian Network
and author of *Integral Christianity: The Spirit's Call to Evolve*


"Spirit X is an elegant and beautifully written kaleidoscope of the aspects of spiritual principle, paths and practices. It feels simple because it has integrated complexity so well. It is playful and clear, gentle and open. It embraces the many expressions of faith that we have. It is an invitation to growth which is compatible with the work of Ken Wilber, and of the developmentalists. It is a pleasure to endorse Spirit X."

—Cindy Wigglesworth
author of *SQ21: The Twenty-One Skills of Spiritual Intelligence*
President of Deep Change, Inc.

"It's funny. Anandamali wrote Spirit X and asked me to review the book. It was delivered to me via hardcopy in a purple Mead brand folder, which itself had "Five Star" as a logo written on it. I know, not so funny so far—not until I went to write this review and wanted to say something about the book. And all that came up initially was CELEBRATION: "Five Star!!!". Yes, "Five Stars out of 5 stars," for the integrity, honesty and know-how given to this matter of spirituality in today's integration of it called Spirit X. Anandamali let's you have it. All of it. And the "I" and "We", too, in this "Five Star!!!" production."

—Mokshananda,
spiritual teacher at Free Water Sangha

"In Spirit X, Ananda skillfully translates ancient spiritual wisdom for the modern era. Using short, pithy chapters to deliver his teachings, Ananda weaves dharma, practice, and the evolution of consciousness into a seamless declaration of an integral spirituality for our digital age. Spirit X is one of those books that you can pick up and read anywhere and anytime. Readers are sure to benefit from the gems of wisdom it contains."

—Dustin DiPerna, author of *Streams of Wisdom*

"Nikola Ristic has written a multi-faceted, playful, creative, and expansive guide to spiritual growth. There is spiritual wisdom and nurturance here for people at every step along the path."

—Mark Forman, PhD,
author of *The Monster's Journey: From Trauma to Connection*

"A timely deep dive into spirituality with a very rich overview on the many inroads to the depth of your own consciousness. I highly recommend this read from Nikola, who is a unique guide with integral awareness."

—Bence Ganti
integral psychologist,
founder of Integral Academy and
the Integral European Conferences (IEC)

"Nikola Ristic offers an integral approach for contemporary seekers to discover their True Nature and express it with gusto. There are a thousand ways to kneel and kiss the ground. Spirit X helps you to find yours and become a blessing to others."

— Dennis Wittrock
co-founder Integral European Conference

# SPIRIT X

## Spirituality for the Global & Digital Age

## BASIC PRINCIPLES

Nikola Anandamali Ristic

It is advisable that practices and principles from this book are practiced with qualified teachers, mentors and spiritual communities. Practices and principles from this book are not a diagnosis or advice for any kind of medical, psychological, emotional or spiritual problems.

✱

Spirit X: Spirituality for the Global and Digital Age—Basic Principles

ISBN: 978-0-578-79017-6

Copyright © 2021 Nikola Ristic

All rights reserved. No parts of this book may be reproduced without prior written permission from the publisher

Published by Spirit X Publications

Second Edition

Printed and Bound in the United States of America

Cover design by Carrie Toder imagics.com
Layout and design by Brad Reynolds integralartandstudies.com
Photo by Tracy Rasmussen

For more information about Spirit X and Nikola Anandamali Ristic see: anandamali.com

# Table of Contents

Introduction ................................................................ vii

# SPIRIT X 1.0

## PART 1: The Self

#1 Pause ........................................................................ 1
#2 Breathe ..................................................................... 4
#3 Salute Yourself, Others and the World ....................... 7
#4 You Can Do This and Be That ................................. 11
#5 Freedom and Happiness Are Your Birthright .......... 15
#6 Practice ................................................................... 17
#7 Open Yourself to Grace ........................................... 20
#8 Spiritual Practice Is Neither Difficult Nor Easy, It Is Just Tricky ............................................................... 26
#9 Ego-Transcendence Is the Cornerstone of Genuine Spiritual Practice ..................................................... 28
#10 Spirit Has Two Dimensions: Unmanifest and Manifest .................................................................. 33
#11 Major Spiritual Practices Given to Us by the Wisdom Traditions Are Meditation, Prayer, Contemplation, Inquiry, Satsang, Kirtan, Yoga, Movement, Dance and Silence ................................. 36
#12 Science and Technology Are Opening New Ways to Practice Spirituality in the Modern World ......... 41

#13 Body and Mind Are Important on the Spiritual Journey ........................................................ 46

#14 Align with Your Relative Purpose and Fulfill Your Absolute Purpose .................................................. 56

#15 Connect with Your Soul ........................................... 60

#16 Realize Your True Self .............................................. 66

#17 Death Is a Transition ............................................... 75

## PART II: THE WORLD

#18 Like Spirit, Reality Has Two Dimensions: Unmanifest and Manifest ......................................... 81

#19 Manifest Reality Is Multidimensional and a Spectrum ............................................................ 83

#20 Unmanifest Reality Is Beyond Space and Time, and Beyond the Cycle of Birth, Death and Rebirth ...... 85

#21 The World Is a Place to Make an Effort Towards Ego-Transcendence, Wisdom and Love, and Self-Realization ...................................................... 88

#22 Connect with Others ................................................ 90

#23 Commune with Nature ............................................ 93

#24 Relationships and Sex Are Means for Spiritual Growth and Unfolding ............................................ 97

#25 Work, Career and Money Are Means for Spiritual Growth and Unfolding .......................................... 102

#26 Culture and Pop-Culture Are Means for Spiritual Growth and Unfolding .......................................... 110

## Table of Contents

#27 Art Is a Means for Spiritual Growth and Unfolding ............... 116

#28 Utilize Science for Your Spiritual Growth and Unfolding ............... 119

#29 Utilize Technology for Your Spiritual Growth and Unfolding ............... 122

#30 Transform Your Relationship to Negativity ........... 126

#31 Overcome Materialism ....................... 130

#32 Own Your Power ............................. 136

#33 Don't Get Distracted ........................ 141

#34 Spirit X 1.0 Reading Completion Congratulations! ........................ 143

#35 Commercials 1.0 ............................. 144

# SPIRIT X 2.0
## PART III: THE BOOK OF WAYS

#36 Ways and Codes ............................. 151

#37 Master Ways .................................. 153

#38 The Way of Meditation ..................... 160

#39 The Way of Awareness ..................... 166

#40 The Way of Spiritual Warrior ............. 173

#41 The Way of the Trickster .................. 178

#42 The Way of Beauty ......................... 186

#43 The Way of Mahavatar Babaji ........... 191

#44 The Way of Shiva ........................... 204

#45 The Way of Madonna, the Holy Mother ............ 217
#46 The Way of Wilber ................................................. 227
#47 The Way of the Spiritual Muse ........................... 250
#48 Ways Are Infinite .................................................. 257

## Part IV: The Book of Codes

#49 Codes and Ways ................................................... 261
#50 Master Codes ....................................................... 262
#51 Child Code ........................................................... 268
#52 Woman Code ....................................................... 272
#53 Man Code ............................................................. 277
#54 We-the-People Code ............................................ 283
#55 Holistic Code ....................................................... 287
#56 Achiever Code ..................................................... 294
#57 Player Code .......................................................... 298
#58 Hacker Code ........................................................ 304
#59 Hipster Code ........................................................ 308
#60 60's Code .............................................................. 314
#61 Mediterranean Code ............................................ 321
#62 Madonna, Queen of Pop Code ........................... 328
#63 Codes Are Infinite ................................................ 336
#64 Spirit X 2.0 Reading Completion
    Congratulations! ..................................................... 337
#65 Commercials 2.0 .................................................. 338

# Table of Contents

## Outroduction

#66 Silence ................................................................ 343
#67 Word .................................................................. 344
#68 Not of This World ............................................. 345
#69 Shiva's Hand Is Raised ....................................... 346

SPIRIT X

# Introduction

Here we are, my friend.

Here, individually, in the human condition, identified with the mind-body, in a world we are trying to make sense of.

And, Here we are, collectively, together in the human dimension during both challenging and inspiring times. In many areas of our lives, such as health, economy and environment, we are facing a major crisis. In many other areas, such as technology, science and spirituality we are witnessing amazing progress. As a species, we are in a major transition. Worlds are appearing, shining and disappearing in front of our eyes. We are entering the Age of Transformation, where crisis and evolution are simultaneous: good things are getting better, worse things are getting worse and fast things are getting faster. As such, this age requires from us a major reset of our minds, hearts, and togetherness, and a profound reconsideration of who we truly are.

And, Here we are, ultimately, in the timeless Here and Now, beyond the karma of body, mind and the world, beyond samsaric cycle of birth, death and rebirth, in the Here and Now that is our true being and Home. This Here and Now still awaits its full realization and utilization and that is certainly something to work on and look forward to.

So what would a spirituality for our age look like? A spirituality that honors the best from East and West, the wisdom traditions such as Christianity, Hinduism, Buddhism, Islam, and Taoism and the legacies of the modern world such as democracy, science and technology. A spirituality that integrates wisdom, knowledge, nature, culture, arts, pop-culture and much more. Or, even wider put, a spirituality that is a true East-West-North-South global synthesis, blending and utilizing together the ancientness and spirit of the East, reason and practicality of the West, executiveness and structure of the North and spontaneity and warmth of the South. A spirituality that rests upon and honors the past, creates a future that is bringing us closer to our Divinity and is grounded in the Ultimate Present. And, finally, a popular spirituality that is deep, efficient, funny and that works. Spirit X is an attempt to answer that call. It is an upgrade of the Dharma, a spiritual teaching that is truly global and that utilizes the digital age, a teaching designed for the 21st century practitioner and beyond.

A few words about the structure of the book. It consist of two levels, Spirit X 1.0 and Spirit X 2.0, and four parts, The Self, The World, The Book of Ways and The Book of Codes. Spirit X 1.0 (Part 1, The Self and Part 2, The World) is an experiential synthesis of the emerging global spirituality. Emphasis is placed on wisdom, knowledge and practices that are suitable for and respond to our global and digital age. Spirit X 2.0 (Part 3, The Book of Ways and Part 4, The Book of Codes) is a living multidimensional embodiment of both our relative and ultimate being, and, as such, an open-ended, co-creative, ever-evolving, playful synthesis of East-West-North-South global spirituality. As our accelerated transformation, that is, crisis-evolution, continues, Spirit X and its further levels and versions will be here to continue supporting our individual and collective spiritual life and evolution.

How to read this book? The principles in this book include philosophical explanations, meditations, prayers, contemplations, non-dual pointers, spiritual poetry, energetic frequencies, empowerments, trickster jokes and much more. At its core, the principles are reminders of the richness of the human dimension and cosmos. My wish is that the reader reads this book not necessarily with the mind but with the Heart, with one's whole Being. As we are approaching a trans-rational and trans-egoic age, reading a book with an open Heart and full Being is becoming the new way of reading.

I wrote this book in Santa Cruz, CA. My feeling is that this mind-body would never have had this kind of insight and inspiration anywhere else in the world. I felt that, creatively, I was at the right place at the right time. Santa Cruz appeared to me like the Beach of the World, like a confluence of Life and Spirit, like an evolutionary frontier of the global world. The Sky, Ocean and Mountains seamlessly blended together into a Cosmic Whole, nature and culture danced in higher Unity; agriculture, technology and spirituality were all progressing almost effortlessly to the next level. And, indeed, the tensions, wounds and pathologies of the global world were making themselves visible and calling for healing and reconciliation.

# Spirit X

Above everything else, in Santa Cruz I witnessed Beauty beyond human realm and rested in the Unknown, pregnant with possibilities.

I am deeply grateful to have spent this part on my life on the American West Coast and for the insight and inspiration I received here. May they serve the well-being, healing and Awakening of All.

Here we are, my friend!

Here!?

Santa Cruz, CA, June 2020

# SPIRIT X

## Spirituality for the Global & Digital Age

## BASIC PRINCIPLES

# SPIRIT X 1.0

To the Ones who suffer, yet intuit that there is a way out of suffering.

To the Ones inspired to practice wholeheartedly.

To the Ones ready to utilize a spirituality of our global age.

To the Ones I Love.

# Part I
# The Self

Spirit X

# #1
# PAUSE

Hush. Now.

Spiritual life starts with a pause—a Holy Pause—with slowing down of the body, the mind and the world. Modern living is characterized by high speed, complexity and overwhelm which overshadows the deeper dimension of our being, our higher potential and our True Self. When we pause, we slow down the karma of the body, the mind and the world and get ready to explore the deeper dimension of our being and Reality. The best kind of pause is produced by engaging with numerous spiritual practices such as meditation, prayer, contemplation, satsang, yoga, communing with nature, connecting with others, using technology for spiritual purposes, etc. Modern living and spiritual living don't exclude each other; on the contrary, it is very possible and even advisable to live a spiritual life while fully engaged with the various dimensions of the modern world. This meaningful and creative engagement adds fullness to a spiritual life.

∞

Take a break for a moment from what you are doing. Slow down your body and mind, soften your relationship with the world.

# Spirit X

What is really going on Here? Why are you Here? Who are you, really? What is your relationship to others and the world? Is there a God and what is your relationship with That? What happens to us when we die? Notice what happens to your mind-body when you open to these deeper philosophical and spiritual questions.

Although questions like these may seem reserved only for those interested in philosophical, existential and spiritual issues, in the present day world, those questions are becoming a prerequisite for navigating our rich and complex world and living a meaningful, happy and fulfilling life.

∞

Take a pause on your own and share that pause with others. Notice how slowing down connects you with yourself, others and the world. Notice how joint slowing down influences human interaction and brings forward an irresistible bond.

∞

When body, mind and world rest, you connect with your soul. Live from that place.

∞

When body, mind and world rest you connect with others, world and Divine on a deeper level. Explore this depth.

∞

When body, mind and world rest, Gods and Goddesses are expressing themselves in this realm through you. Be this noble vehicle.

∞

When body, mind and world rest, Awareness shines. Be that pure Light.

∞

"He who dies with the most toys wins." Did we get this right, my friend? Did we get this right?

∞

Hush.

∞

Take a Holy Pause.

# #2
# BREATHE

*Inhale. Exhale.*

Breath has been a doorway to a deeper dimension of our being and to Presence for centuries. With various breathing techniques we dis-identify with the body, the mind and whatever situation we are in. When we breathe consciously we get centered and prepare the mind-body for deeper dissolving back into Presence, Peace and Stillness. Breathing also activates our subtle-energetic body, reveals the fullness of our being and brings us closer to our True Self. Breath is a reminder that we are much more than what we think we are and that Reality is much more than we think it is.

☙

What is the quality of your breath right now? Fast? Slow? Shallow? Deep? Natural? Unaware? By noticing the quality of your breath in various situations—both within and without—you are opening a space for deeper intimacy, knowing and mastery of the inner and outer universes.

☙

Take a deep breath, into the belly and out. Repeat several times. Notice how the sense of self and the sense of the world change after just a few breaths. Notice the body relaxing, the mind slowing down or even fully stopping. How incredible—only a few breaths and everything changed and transformed. Stay centered, clear and energized. Deepen your inquiry.

☙

Take a deep breath. Exhale. Notice how, all of a sudden, everything is much more peaceful and clear. Be that Peace and Clarity.

☙

Across the spiritual traditions, there are numerous breathing techniques readily available to us in our global world. Whether you count your breath in order to strengthen your concentration, or breathe to calm down and let go, or breathe to activate the subtle-energy body, breathing is the best introduction to spirituality and for deeper inquiry and release.

☙

Inhale—connect with the Presence.
Exhale—release the karma of body, mind and world.

Inhale—it's all OK.
Exhale—it's all OK.

Inhale—acknowledge the universe Within.
Exhale—embrace the universe Without.

# Spirit X

Inhale—the world dissolves into nothingness.
Exhale—the world is created.

Inhale—I am Nothing.
Exhale—I am Everything.

Inhale—you are Free and Still.
Exhale—you are Free and Radiant.

Inhale—you are YourSelf.
Exhale—you are YourSelf.

☙

Go back to the breath again and again and again…

☙

Or, as we see today on many T-shirts and many posts on social networks —"Breathe!"

☙

Ultimately, breathing releases us into the part of our being and Reality that is beyond breath. What is that in you—and in Reality—that does not need breath for its own existence. Be That.

# #3
# SALUTE YOURSELF, OTHERS AND THE WORLD

Put your palms together, send honoring, loving attention to yourself, your birth and your human condition.

Put your palms together, acknowledge others on the path and send them honoring, loving attention.

Put your palms together, acknowledge the world in its many perspectives and dimensions and send it honoring, loving attention.

Honor yourself, your separate, human self. Human birth is precious and a result of good deeds and karma. In human, relative form, you—and all other human beings—are given the opportunity to re-discover your absolute, formless Self, your True Self, your True Nature. Honor yourself in this precious human form. Cultivate the practice of honoring yourself in the form of bowing, gratitude, visualizations and whatever practice works for you.

When we suggest here to salute and honor yourself, your

# Spirit X

relative self, the point is not to strengthen the ego, the sense of separate self. The point is to acknowledge—both cognitively and experientially—the full spectrum of your Self, from ego to soul to True Self. Human birth is an amazing opportunity to realize and be this full spectrum with the climax being Self-Realization. Honor this opportunity. It is more than available to us in our contemporary world.

Bow to yourself first thing in the morning and last thing in the evening.

Start the day with five grateful thoughts about being in human form or keep a gratitude journal about living in the human condition.

Close your eyes, visualize your human form held and supported by divine Spirit. How not to be grateful for being born in human form?

Honor others you meet on your path. We are here to help each other find a way back Home. At times we do it wisely and lovingly, at times we do it fiercely, and at times we do it clumsily and imperfectly. The point is that we are all in this together. On a deeper level, there is no spiritual growth without a loving and supportive spiritual community.

Bow to others. Look them gently in the eyes. Acknowledge the Divine in them.

Honor various perspectives and expressions of Spirit within the manifest world such as nature, culture, society, human evolution, education, technological structure, etc. On a deeper level, the world is Here to support our spiritual growth. Commune with nature, be grateful for our planet, our home. Implement some environmental practices into your life. Acknowledge the cultural ideas and values that you share with others. It is incredible that we can resonate with each other on that level and go deeper together. Acknowledge what we call civilization or human history or human evolution. We have come a long way together. We are standing on the shoulders of the giants of human evolution. How not to be grateful? Connect with others on the Internet and in virtual space. Be grateful for technology bringing us together into a global community and offering us the tools for well-being, transformation and awakening.

Acknowledge the divinity of the world. Notice the Divine in your breath, in the sip of coffee going down your throat,

# Spirit X

in the eyes of the other, in a child's laughter, in the morning sun, in the afternoon rain, in your favorite song, in the sky, in deep meditation, during lovemaking, in your dreams, in dreamless sleep.

Close your eyes. Feel the world in its many perspectives and dimensions supporting your spiritual growth.

Bow to the world, in all of its richness.

Be grateful. Be Gratitude.

# #4
# You Can Do This and Be That

Spiritual empowerment is a bit different than empowerment in other areas of the human condition. It is about re-membering and re-discovering who and what you already are. It is more about dis-identifying than achieving, more about accepting and allowing what is than about fixing, pushing and striving.

Further in the book, we will see that spiritual growth and unfolding includes our body, mind and spirit as well as the multidimensionality of our being and Reality. Within that, some relative empowerments (body, mind, work, etc) are appropriate. In this principle, however, we are focused on genuine spiritual empowerment which is different in nature than relative empowerment.

One of the most important and effective spiritual pointers and instructions can be found in the *Upanishads*, within the Hindu tradition: Thou art That. You are That. What you are seeking, you already are. Atman, your individual essence, is identical to Brahman, the essence of Reality. You are already that what you are seeking, wanting and striving for. The matter is only to shift your attention and realize That. And, indeed, be That. Spiritual empowerment is not about achieving something but rather re-discovering That that you already are.

You are already That, the Self. Every human being is already That, the Self. The whole reality is already That, the Self. If you are already That, then whether you deserve it or not is out of the question. It's just a matter of shifting your attention and re-membering who and what you truly are. Why wouldn't you be able to do it?

Of course, the momentum of egoic conditioning is strong and a simple pointer like this is often not enough. It takes effort, practice and grace to realize That, the Self. But this pointer is a powerful spiritual encouragement, too. You are already That—one just needs to peel the onion of one's being and realize, be and express That. And in the present day and age—with all the spiritual techniques available to us today—it is not as difficult a task as it used to be.

It is often thought that spirituality and especially its most precious jewel Enlightenment or Self-Realization—realization of and being That—is reserved only for masters, sages and special ones, the ones who had the karmic privilege of being spiritually advanced. Lately, with the democratization of many resources, ideas and values here on planet Earth, things have radically changed with spirituality, too. Spirituality and Enlightenment are no longer reserved only for advanced ones and special ones but are everyone's right and possibility.

At the beginning of your spiritual path, give yourself a dosage of spiritual empowerment. You can do this thing called spiritual growth and unfolding. You can achieve Enlightenment in this lifetime. Resources are richer for spiritual growth than in any other time in history, and you are supported in it by others and the universe. And, most importantly, you are already That, it's just a matter of shifting attention, seeing through and peeling the onion of your being.

Surround yourself with friends and conditions that are empowering you. You can do this and be That.

In our time and age, spiritual growth and unfolding—and even Enlightenment—is becoming an evolutionary necessity. In a world that is at times beautiful and at times overwhelmingly complex, where fast is faster, worse is worse and better is better, our spiritual growth and Enlightenment are becoming an imperative. You can do this, and be That, because evolution needs you to.

Ultimately—you are already That. And this is the highest form of empowerment one can get in human form.

# #5
# Freedom and Happiness Are Your Birthright

In the human condition, we are born with certain rights: human, civil, ethical, legal, etc. And, as we mature, grow and become more responsible, we earn more rights. If our rights are violated we claim them and we expect others and society to protect our rights. There is quite a human wisdom in that. There are however, spiritual rights too, or even better put, spiritual birthrights. One of the tricks at the beginning of your spiritual journey is to claim your spiritual birthright to freedom and happiness.

This book is like a little contract between you the reader, and me the author. By reading this book, you give me your attention, you trust me, you allow me to open something deeper and higher in you, you give me permission to be your teacher or guide. If everything goes well, you will taste Freedom, Happiness and Bliss of Being which does not depend on any external objects and phenomena and help others do the same. But the trick is that you cannot force people to be free. Me wanting you to be free is not enough. You need to want your Freedom. And it all starts with claiming your birthright to Freedom and Happiness.

# Spirit X

Say gently: "This lifetime is the lifetime when I am going to fully realize Freedom and Happiness inherent to my being and Reality." Let this statement echo in every corner of your being and Reality.

Say gently: "I claim my spiritual birthright to Freedom and Fulfillment." Let this statement echo in every corner of your being and Reality.

Say gently:" I deserve Freedom and Happiness." Let this statement echo in every corner of your being and Reality.

✛

Once born in the human condition you are born with a spiritual right and spiritual endowment. At the core of your being you are Free and Happy. Claim you birthright. Make an effort and allow Grace to realize That, be and express That and, indeed, help others realize and be That.

# # 6
# PRACTICE

Spiritual practice is a movement from identifying with our egoic, separate self to re-discovering, resting and living as our True Self. Throughout the centuries and across wisdom traditions, we have been given numerous powerful and effective spiritual practices, such as meditation, prayer, contemplation, satsang, yoga, dance, etc. We are fortunate to have all of these practices available to us today. Be grateful for their existence, their availability, experiment with them and stick to the practices that produce the best results for you.

Spiritual practice is best done in a proper spiritual container. The Buddhist tradition emphasizes the three jewels and refuges: Buddha, Dharma and Sangha. Buddha refers to the awakened awareness in Buddha and each of us. Dharma is the teaching that reveals the ultimate nature of Reality. Sangha is the group of spiritual practitioners supporting each other in the pursuit and realization of the Truth.

Applied to the contemporary spiritual situation Buddha, Dharma and Sangha are the following: Buddha is the awakened awareness in yourself and your teacher or mentor. Make an effort to realize awakened awareness on your own and allow qualified teachers and mentors to help you.

# Spirit X

Practice on your own and work with a teacher or mentor.

Dharma in the contemporary context is a set of teachings that reveal to us ultimate and relative reality. For ultimate reality, we have traditional spiritual teachings (Christianity, Buddhism, Hinduism, Islam, Taoism) and contemporary nonduality. For relative reality, we have rich discourses produced by the modern and contemporary world, such as psychology, philosophy, science and technology, pop-culture, self-help, new age spirituality, etc. We definitely don't lack teachings in the present day world.

Finally, Sangha in the contemporary context are spiritual groups of like-minded people that support each other in the process of spiritual growth and unfolding. Find a Sangha that works for you. Get support and give support. The vast majority of 21st century spiritual practitioners belong to multiple Sanghas—that's fine, as long as the process doesn't become overwhelming and confusing.

One of the most important things about practice is regularity. If you find that meditation works for you—do it regularly. If you pray—do it regularly. With regularity, the more you practice, the more you release karma, let go of attachments, have a liberating insight, feel more love and compassion for yourself and others, dis-identify from your small, relative self, and rest more as your True Self. With regular practice, you create a second nature beyond your ego and eventually as your True Self. The right container for spiritual practice always relies on regularity.

In the beginning stages of spiritual practice there is a gap between practice and life. Practice feels good and meaningful while life feels difficult and challenging. It takes a bit of practice to keep the spiritual frequency throughout our daily lives, with all the ups and downs inherent to it. Eventually, you realize that the real goal of spiritual practice is the end of practice and the beginning of effortless spiritual life, or simply Life.

Practice until there is no boundary between practice and life. Then—simply Be.

May you find Buddha, Dharma and Sangha and realize your True Self.

Spirit X

# # 7
# Open Yourself to Grace

Although practice can be very spiritually empowering and efficient, it is often not enough. The highest form of practice is surrender to Grace, simply trusting the process of spiritual unfolding, receiving a higher Power, and accepting what is.

Grace is a simple acknowledgment and surrender to something bigger than ourselves within and without. You can call it Higher Power, or the Divine, or God, or Goddess, or Awareness, or whatever works for you. The key is acknowledging that you are not alone on your spiritual journey or in life in general. You are supported and guided in it. Grace can be gentle or fierce, clear or mysterious, we can easily recognize it and accept it or struggle to do so. It can take many forms, from the help we get from our family and friends (and even pets), to meeting someone who changes our life, to revealing insight, to getting hooked on spiritual practice, to Divine vision, to spiritual Enlightenment. It may also take seemingly negative forms such as loss of a job, a devastating breakup, a disease, war, natural disasters, experiencing a collective crisis, feeling alone on the path, the loss of someone dear to us and our own death.

Empty-Luminous Formless Field
Everything that ever existed is There
Everything that will ever exist is There
Every tear, every laughter
Every birth and every death
Grace.

In the beginning, there is Grace
In the middle, there is Grace
At the end, there is Grace
It's Grace all the Way, my friend.

Birth: Here you are again
Forgetting who you are and why you came
Yet gradually remembering.
Being born in precious human condition
What an opportunity
What a grace.

In the beginning, there is Grace
In the middle, there is Grace
At the end, there is Grace
It's Grace all the Way, my friend.

You are a child
You are happy when you get what you want
You are unhappy when you don't get what you want

# Spirit X

Yet the energy is boundless
And the world is a place of Wonder
What a Grace.

In the beginning, there is Grace
In the middle, there is Grace
At the end, there is Grace
It's Grace all the Way, my friend.

Teenage years are times to rebel
To differentiate
And establish yourself as a unique individual
Pushing the boundaries, building your own core
Good moments, tough moments
Grace.

In the beginning, there is Grace
In the middle, there is Grace
At the end, there is Grace
It's Grace all the Way, my friend.

Life is good, Life is bad
Lots of ups and downs
Lots of winning and losing
It's tough
But somewhere deep you know
There must be some deeper
Peace and Bliss in all of this.
Grace, is that you?
Grace, where are you?

## Open Yourself to Grace

In the beginning, there is Grace
In the middle, there is Grace
At the end, there is Grace
It's Grace all the Way, my friend.

And then, one day you realize the importance of Spirit
And become a spiritual practitioner
You practice
You practice hard
Practice feels good, life feels challenging
Yet, it's only Grace.

In the beginning, there is Grace
In the middle, there is Grace
At the end, there is Grace
It's Grace all the Way, my friend.

And then, it happens
You die before your physical death
Spirit sees itself as Spirit
Through you as a pure vehicle
It was all a Dream
What Grace!

In the beginning, there is Grace
In the middle, there is Grace
At the end, there is Grace
It's Grace all the Way, my friend.

Since I have seen
I will help others do the same

# Spirit X

Spirit, I serve You
Giving is endless Regeneration in the Now
The highest Grace.

In the beginning, there is Grace
In the middle, there is Grace
At the end, there is Grace
It's Grace all the Way, my friend.

Death: taking off of mind-body
Release without fear and remorse
Empty-Luminous Formless Field
Another Name for You
Reincarnation or Final Liberation
It's all Grace anyways.

In the beginning, there is Grace
In the middle, there is Grace
At the end, there is Grace
It's Grace all the Way.

It's Grace all the Way
My Friend

Through Grace we understand and feel that we are supported by the universe and the Divine in our spiritual growth and unfolding. Through Grace and its support, love, and intelligence, we are given help and guidance to transcend our separate self and to realize our True Self.

# Open Yourself to Grace

May you realize Grace within, without and beyond.

# #8
# Spiritual Practice is Neither Difficult Nor Easy, It Is Just Tricky

The whole process we call spiritual practice is not difficult. If you practice in the right container and open yourself to Grace—you will experience long lasting results. Spiritual practice is, also, not easy, since many practitioners struggle with it, get stuck, and don't achieve desirable result.

The best way to describe spiritual practice is to say that it is tricky. We start practicing with a strong feeling that we are missing something essential, that we need to go somewhere else or be somebody else in order to be spiritual and enlightened. One of the biggest traps and yet necessary stages of spiritual practice is seeking and ascending. We seek God, Enlightenment, Peace, Bliss and Unity. We ascend into higher and more subtle realms of our own being and Reality. The biggest trick to spiritual practice is to stop seeking, to stop identifying with the seeker, and to simply rest and investigate what is present Here and Now.

Who IS right Here and Now? Who is AWARE right Here,

right Now? Be That. Realizing That is the end of seeking (and practice). And the beginning of the Expression of That in human form and realm (and the beginning of service).

The best way to address this trickiness of spiritual unfolding is to practice on your own, work with the qualified teacher or mentor, and practice with supportive and qualified Sangha. Some spiritual practices work with the form (such as counting breath, concentration techniques, visualizations) and some spiritual practices resolve seeking and release us into the formless (such as formless meditation, self-inquiry and satsang). The vast majority of spiritual practitioners need to work with a teacher or mentor wholeheartedly in order to dissolve seeking, whether it be inherent to human condition or spiritual in nature.

Who and What is AWARE, right Here, right Now?

# #9

# Ego-Transcendence Is the Cornerstone of Genuine Spiritual Practice

At the depths of your being, my friend, there is an intuition that you are much more than the mind-body, that you have a soul, that your potential is infinite, that somehow you are one with God already. Trust that intuition, my friend, and it will take you to places that mind cannot comprehend.

≈

Ego in spirituality is a false sense of self, it is what we think we are and not what we really are. It is based on centering one's being upon the sense of I-me-mine. The ego comes into existence when we attach the thought of "I" to the body and add to it our life-story, values, ideas, likes and dislikes, suffering, disappointments, hopes, fears, good and bad attachments, good and bad habits, memories from the past and anticipations of the future. Ego-identification comes with a strong sense of separation from others and the world. And, any sense of separation brings with itself an inherent suffering. The logic behind that suffering is: if there is something other than me, I must either want it or fear it. And that's how the loop of ego-identification starts. At its core, ego is a sense of lack and a point of resistance to what is. For more Abundance, Peace, Love, Bliss and Creativity, ego-transcendence is necessary.

≈

From a spiritual standpoint, one of the major spiritual limits of ego-identification is that it is inherently narcissistic. Narcissus is a figure from Greek mythology who fell in love with his image in the water and, as a result, got degraded into a flower. Without going into discussing narcissism here as a psychological pathology, let us notice an inherently narcissistic tendency in ego-identification as such: an obsession with I-me-mine.

≈

There is quite a bit of confusion when it comes to ego in spirituality, even in the wisdom traditions. Often we hear statements like "Ego is the enemy," or instructions like "Kill the ego," or "Get rid of ego." For some reason, ego got a very bad reputation in spirituality. However, in trying to get rid of something or even kill it, you are just reinforcing it. Genuine spirituality is the game of witnessing, allowing phenomena to be, come and go, welcoming both "good" and "bad" experiences, being friends with the "positive" and "negative." Only that way we can become what we truly are, our True Self, free, radiant and creative. That's why

# Spirit X

by ego-transcendence here we don't mean transcend and get rid of ego, or repress the ego, but transcend and include the ego into the deeper spectrum of your being, which includes the ego, the soul and the True Self (and many other possible stages in between).

≈

The best way to transcend and include ego is to see-through and feel-through the egoic structure. That which sees the ego is the Eye of Spirit. And that seeing is freeing. That which feels the ego is the Sentience of Spirit. And that feeling is freeing. Many spiritual practices across traditions, practices and tools from science and technology, as well as states of consciousness that are spontaneously available to us in the human condition, help this process.

≈

Notice when you get defensive, notice when you want to be right, notice when you are reacting, rather than responding, notice when you argue with Reality wishing things to be different (sometimes just for the sake of arguing), notice when you are lacking this or that. Feel through all of it.

≈

Trust me, my friend, once you see-through and feel-through the egoic structure you won't be interested in playing egoic games any more.

## Ego-Transcendence

≈

We usually take the ego to be an entity when, in fact, it is an activity—a loop of thoughts, feelings, sensations, interpretations, stories, judgements, plans, aspirations, reactions to life-circumstances, hopes and fears. It comes and goes, it arises, shines and dissolves. It is our mind and cultural custom that make it an entity.

≈

We also assume that we are in ego all the time, yet we are often in trans-egoic states of consciousness. Think of doing what you love, contemplating a work of art, communing with nature, making love, listening to your favorite song, not to mention while we are sleeping.

≈

Where is your ego in deep dreamless sleep, my friend?

≈

Body sensations come and go, thoughts come and go, ego-identification comes and goes.

≈

You have an ego, you have a soul, you are the Self.

≈

# Spirit X

What is the promise of ego-transcendence? More Peace, Love, Enthusiasm, Insight, and, most importantly, less arguing with Reality over what you seemingly lack.

≈

The thing is, my friend, the spiritual cheesecake is beyond the ego. Simply do it. Any ego-based religion or spirituality just reinforces the sense of lack and separation.

≈

There are numerous practices, activities and states of consciousness that can help you transcend—and include—your ego. From meditation, prayer and contemplation, to doing what you love, to communing with nature and listening your favorite song, to the natural sleep cycle (waking, dreaming, deep dreamless sleep)—ego transcendence is easier than it looks and, an absolutely necessary step in spiritual unfolding and both individual and collective evolution. From a spiritual standpoint, the key is to make the ego an ambassador of the Spirit in the human dimension by making it spiritually transparent, psychologically healthy, rationally wide and practically engaged with the world in the name of transformation and evolution of consciousness.

≈

You have an ego, you are the Self.

# #10
# Spirit Has Two Dimensions: Unmanifest and Manifest

Spirit is Everything and Nothing, it is in everything and everywhere and beyond it. It is impossible to understand it fully mentally and to express it fully in language. Although One (or better put, Not-Two), the best way to understand Spirit cognitively and to experience it spiritually is to recognize that there are two basic dimensions of Spirit: unmanifest and manifest, ultimate and relative. The unmanifest dimension of Spirit is beyond this universe, beyond birth, death and rebirth, beyond space and time, it is Absolute Subjectivity and Freedom. The manifest dimension of Spirit consists of myriad forms and levels of Spirit in this universe and infinite other universes.

Recent discoveries in science and spirituality reveal to us an important fact about relative reality: it evolves and grows. It is the movement from matter to life to mind to soul to spirit. In various structures and systems, evolutionary patterns can be recognized and applied. For instance, human life can be seen as an evolution from birth to spiritual enlightenment. The significance of an evolutionary, developmental view of spirituality is essential: we can see our individual and collective life as an evolution towards our Divinity.

The realization and teaching offered to us by various wisdom traditions—Christianity, Hinduism, Buddhism, Islam, Taoism—that an essential part of our being and Reality is beyond body, mind and the world and that it can be pointed to and tasted fully, is the single most important pointer and teaching that has happened on this planet. We come into this dimension to taste freedom in various dimensions and perspectives of the human condition. The most distinguished feature of these teachings is that ultimate freedom can be realized and lived only in the dimensionless dimension of the Unmanifest ( which holds, embraces and is One with the manifest reality). Early Indian sages, Buddha, Jesus, Lao Tzu and many other wise men and women offered us this most precious gift. It is time this gift is fully utilized.

Spirit X as a teaching acknowledges the importance of both unmanifest and manifest dimensions of Spirit and honors teachings that point to unmanifest reality and as well as understand manifest, relative reality. In Spirit X, to realize unmanifest Spirit we master Ways; to see, understand and navigate manifest, relative reality we master Codes.

# #11
# Major Spiritual Practices Given to Us by the Wisdom Traditions Are Meditation, Prayer, Contemplation, Forgiveness, Satsang, Kirtan, Yoga, Inquiry, Movement, Dance and Silence

We live in extraordinary times when it comes to the richness of spiritual practices available to us. Buddhism and Hinduism give us various forms of meditation and yoga, Christianity and Islam give us prayer, Hinduism gives us satsang and kirtan, Taoism gives us movement, Sufism gives us ecstatic dancing, almost all wisdom traditions emphasize silence one way or another, etc.

# Major Spiritual Practices

The key thing about spiritual practices is that they provide a direct experience of Spirit in its many dimensions. While major world religions are based on books as their major document and source and faith as their major vehicle, spirituality is rooted in practice that provides a direct experience of Spirit and one's True Self (which is identical to Ultimate Reality).

Meditation is an experience of the I-dimension of Spirit, Spirit as the Ultimate I. Meditation is one of the most spiritually empowering practices on the planet, since it creates a situation where whatever is happening in the outer circumstances, one can always master and take responsibility for the inner being and dimension. The ultimate goal of meditation is to elegantly dissolve the meditator—and the seeming boundary between inner and outer—and reveal our and universal True Self.

Prayer is the experience of the You-dimension of Spirit, Spirit as the Ultimate You or Thou. Spirit in the You-dimension can take the form of God, Goddess, Heavenly Father, Holy Mother, Beloved, Friend, angels, archetypes, guides, other fellow humans, etc. Prayer as a spiritual practice introduces the spiritual dimension between the self and the world and makes the world and our existence in it a more supportive, trusted and loving place.

# Spirit X

Contemplation is the experience of the It-dimension of Spirit, Spirit as the Ultimate It. Spirit in the It-dimension can take forms of Life itself, the Great Chain of Being, multidimensional Cosmos, etc. Spiritual contemplation turns the world into the meaningful whole and the emanation of Spirit.

Forgiveness is the experience of Spirit as empathy, understanding and letting go of resentment towards oneself, others and the world. Forgiveness turns oneself from a victim of life circumstances to a subject of change, growth and evolution and, ultimately, opens avenues towards re-discovery of our True Self.

Satsang is the experience of Spirit as gathering in Truth embodied by the enlightened teacher and devoted practitioners. Traditionally, satsang involves sitting with an enlightened guru and having a discussion about spiritual matters. In a more modern setting, satsang is a fairly informal gathering in which practitioners are invited to inquire into the nature of their self and re-discover their True Self.

Kirtan is the experience of Spirit through devotional sing-

## Major Spiritual Practices

ing. Often done in the call-and-response manner, kirtan uses the power of music, sound and beauty to create a deeper unity among practitioners and release them into the deeper dimension of their own being and Reality.

Yoga is the experience of Spirit through the postures of body, mind and spirit and breathing. Traditionally, yoga has as its final aim the re-discovery of the True Self. In the modern West, yoga is more a practice of body postures with the aim to improve our well-being. In the West, yoga still awaits its full discovery and extension to other parts of our being and Reality.

Inquiry is the experience of Spirit though wholehearted questioning. By asking, for instance, "Who and What am I?", the questioner experientially dissolves into the Source of Being, the Self. The key with inquiry is not to get or understand the answer but to become and embody the answer.

Silence does not mean necessarily the lack of noise but the Silence of Being as the Ground from which everything comes from and where everything goes back. There is Silence, and phenomena arising, shining and dissolving. Silence as a lack of noise certainly helps the discovery of the

39

# Spirit X

Silence of Being, however, it is recommended to contact and rest as the Silence of Being during all activities and circumstances. In the modern world of speed, tension and inner and outer noise, Silence is a spiritual imperative.

Both movement and dance can be used as a deep and effective spiritual practice. Many traditional and modern forms of movement such as Thai Chi, yoga, walking meditations, aikido, hiking, walking the labyrinth, and many traditional and modern forms of dancing such as Sufi whirling, shamanic dance, ecstatic dance, trance dance, kirtan, belly dance, folk circle dance, can be utilized on the spiritual path.

There is no excuse not to practice, my friend. Practices are available, life is rich and can be overwhelming unless we deepen our being and perspective. Please don't listen to the excuses your ego comes up with for not practicing. In the modern world, spiritual practice is becoming an evolutionary and life necessity and, in the years to come, it will be part of the mainstream.

May you... practice.

#12

# SCIENCE AND TECHNOLOGY ARE OPENING NEW WAYS TO PRACTICE SPIRITUALITY IN THE MODERN WORLD

Science and technology are one of the most distinctive features of our global world. They gave us both theoretical frameworks and practical tools to improve our lives. Although their theoretical frameworks can be limited for spiritual unfolding, the practical tools science and technology give us are used more and more for our well-being, spiritual unfolding and even awakening. In this principle, we are focused mostly on the practical aspects and benefits of scientific and technological progress.

The latest discoveries in science and technology give us the opportunity to expand and strengthen our spiritual practice. Smart phones, computers, Internet, biofeedback, neurofeedback, augmented reality, virtual reality and artificial intelligence not only enrich and deepen our practice but also make the process of spiritual growth and enlightenment faster and steadier. Alongside with traditional spiritual practitioner gear such as cushions, statues, incense, images and books, spiritual practitioners of the future will use phones, computers, headphones, oculists, and other technological devices as an everyday tool for their spiritual life.

Utilize the latest scientific discoveries and tools that can improve your well-being and support your spiritual unfolding. With scientific tools spiritual growth can be not only measured but also supplemented, enhanced and accelerated. To mention only few of them: biofeedback brings our mind-body balance, health and function to a higher level, neurofeedback improves the function and activity of the brain, and latest discoveries in correlation between brain waves and states of consciousness open new possibilities to practicing spirituality. Not only that meditative and spiritual states of consciousness change our brain waves, but also, manipulating brain waves we can induce deep, meditative and spiritual states of consciousness. What a relief and what an opportunity.

Transform your relationship with technology and start using it for your well-being and spiritual growth and unfolding. Start with the Holy Trinity of the Digital Age: your smart phone, your computer and the Internet. Be grateful for your smart phone. How incredible it is that someone

## Science and Technology

has invented it and how incredible it is that we can all connect using it. Do you have any content in your phone related to well-being and spirituality? If not—start today. Include your phone in your spiritual toolbox.

Be grateful for your computer. How incredible it is that someone has invented it and that at this point in human evolution we all have an opportunity to use it. Do you use your computer for your well-being and spirituality? And how? If not—start today. Include your computer in your spiritual gear and toolbox, alongside with cushion, statues, images, incense, favorite practices, practitioners and teachers.

Be grateful for the Internet. How incredible it is that the Internet was invented and that we can all use it to browse for information and to connect with each other. Expand yourself by using the Internet. The availability of an abundance of information and global inter-connectivity are basic prerequisites for the Age of Transformation.

Experiment with how new technologies can be used for spiritual growth and unfolding. Just the way you experiment with various meditation techniques and stick to those that produce results, try various technological devices and gadgets, and use them regularly as an integral part of your spiritual practice and life.

# Spirit X

Technology is one of the most sophisticated things we have invented as a species and it would be a shame not to use it for spiritual purposes.

This is not to say that everything regarding science and technology is rainbows and butterflies. We have enough evidence to conclude that science as a worldview and ideology is limited and that overuse of technology can lead to serious problems such as attention problems, alienation, anxiety, depression, addiction, disconnect with the body, exploitation, manipulation, work overload and wealth inequality. The key in using technology for your spiritual growth is moderation and emotional, mental and spiritual discernment.

Would Buddha use the Internet, Facebook and play with virtual reality? There is only one answer to that question.

Since technology is the most developed and sophisticated area of human life at this point in human evolution, the marriage of technology and genuine spirituality can be one of the most important things to influence the future of spirituality, the future of humankind and this planet in general.

## Science and Technology

May we all use the biggest scientific and technological discoveries for the noblest spiritual purposes.

## #13
# BODY AND MIND ARE IMPORTANT ON THE SPIRITUAL JOURNEY

We are holistic and integral beings, we have body, mind and spirit, or, even better put, we have a body, we have a mind and we are essentially Spirit. From an evolutionary perspective body, mind and spirit can be seen as the levels of our being. First we master body, then we master mind and, eventually, we master spirit.

Spiritual growth and unfolding is clearly about Spirit, yet the studies done in the last 30 years show that spiritual growth is faster and steadier if we include the whole of our being into the process. In other words, you will progress spiritually faster and steadier if you practice body, mind and spirit than just practicing spirit. Practically, that means that if, for instance, you eat healthy, run and do yoga (body), read and study (mind) and meditate (spirit), you will progress more spiritually than just by meditating all the time (spirit).

## Body and Mind Are Important

Let's say, you have 20 hours per week exclusively devoted to your spiritual growth and unfolding. It is better and more efficient to do body practices for 5 hours per week, mind practices for 5 hours per week, and spiritual practices for 10 hours per week than to do just spiritual practices for all 20 hours.

Create your own body-mind-spirit cross training. You will be amazed by the results.

Body is the basic level of our being. A healthy, strong and flexible body is a better prerequisite for a spiritual and enlightened life than otherwise. The problem with an unhealthy and dysfunctional body is that it will hijack your attention and create a heavy veil over your ever-present True Self. If you are spending all of your time, energy and money just to heal your body, you will never be able to investigate into the depths of your being and rediscover your True Self. The practices that keep the body strong, healthy and flexible are enough sleep and rest, healthy diet, various kinds of physical exercises, sex, yoga and many more.

From a spiritual standpoint, body is not only the physical body (made of bones, flesh, muscles, nerves and organs) but also the subtle-energy body in its numerous forms (the chakra system, the mind-heart-hara system, koshas (sheaths) system, astral system, Kriya yoga, Taoist macrocosmic orbit, Tantra, kundalini, and many more). The richness of subtle body practices lies in the fact that each subtle body system corresponds to a specific subtle realm of being. With mastering the subtle body we expand and enrich our being. It is imperative to expand the notion of body into the subtle realms for two obvious reasons: the subtle body and realm are the bridge to the ultimate realm of our True Self, and, the next major step in our spiritual evolution will include an explicit awareness and mastery of the subtle realm both individually and collectively.

And, alas, the body dissolves and will dissolve completely. The over-identification with the body leads inevitably to suffering. Thus, practice for the body for Spirit X practitioners means holding the beautiful paradox of the human condition: I keep the body healthy, strong and flexible in spite of the fact that it dissolves and will completely dissolve. I fully honor my body by not over-identifying with it.

The body dissolves—in deep dreamless sleep and after death—what remains? Be That.

Mind is the level of our being that mediates between body

## Body and Mind Are Important

and Spirit. From a spiritual standpoint it is better to approach the mind as a function of Reality, rather than your own individual feature, characteristic or possession. The universal mind finds its own unique expression in you as an individual. Practices for the cultivation of mind include reading, studying, intellectual discussion, psychological work, developing worldview and mindset, traveling, learning foreign languages and more.

Mind is the activity of producing thoughts, judgments, interpretations, stories, images and visions. It is intentional in its nature, it has the capacity to project itself and represent other levels of Reality. Mind can also reflect upon itself but cannot fully see itself.

Close your eyes, my friend. Watch your mind, its thoughts, judgments, stories and images. That which sees the mind is Spirit. It's that simple, my friend.

Mind has two basic functions: analytical and synthetical. Analytical mind operates with opposites (good-bad, right-wrong, I-world, I-you, us-them, etc.). It is what is called in wisdom traditions the dualistic mind. Synthetic mind is a higher function of the mind, as it puts already existing wholes into more meaningful, harmonized and evolutionary wholes (body-mind-spirit unity, transcend-and-inlude evolution, global-transnational world, etc.). A more advanced version of the synthetic mind is the evolutionary or developmental mind which sees the self and reality as developmental systems. Evolutionary mind can be utilized on the spiritual path as a station-like transcend-and-include process towards our individual and collective Divinity. Models in philosophy of German Idealism, developmental psychology, Integral Theory, Aurobindo's Integral Yoga, Gebser's teaching of structures of consciousness and Metamoderna offer maps for the growth of the self and Reality.

In Buddhist tradition they refer to the average human mind as the monkey-mind. Just as a monkey jumps from one branch to another, our untrained mind has a tendency to grab onto various thoughts, feelings, images, judgments and stories. The result is a mental and energetic fatigue that continues the cycle of suffering. The good news is that the human mind—just like the human body—can be trained. One can simply watch the mind with discernment (some thoughts are entertained and some let go of) and adopt the right mindset and the right worldview.

A little experiment: write down every thought of yours for about two hours. You will be surprised how many ridiculous, unnecessary and destructive thoughts can be produced by the human mind.

## Body and Mind Are Important

Adopt the right mindset, my friend. Mindset is a mental attitude and the most optimal interpretation of life and life situations. Mindset is a posture of the mind. When it comes to spiritual growth and unfolding, the right mindset is Trust in the process, belief that you can do it and not overindulging into positive and negative interpretations. As a Zen Master said, interpreting various life situations: "We will see…"

A hint of integral yoga: Assume the right body posture. Assume the right mind posture. Go…

Have the right worldview, my friend. Worldview is simply a lens through which you see and interpret relative reality. There are a myriad of worldviews available within human reality, one can be an environmentalist, athlete, lawyer, poet, feminist, etc. And some worldviews are better than others. It is better to be a communist than a Nazi. And it is better to be a democrat than a communist.

The key question about worldviews is this: Are you aware of your worldview? Or does your worldview unconsciously highjack your mind and attention, obscuring other ways to see and interpret relative reality? Are you stuck in your worldview or can you shift it? Are you aware of other possibilities and worldveiws? Can you see and embody a spectrum of the the worldviews? In Spirit X teaching, spiritual mastery includes playing with and mastering worldviews.

In the present day world there are four dominant cultural worldviews: traditional, modern, post-modern and the new emerging integral worldview. They can be embodied both individually and collectively. The traditional worldview sees and interprets human life and the world through the lens of faith, scripture, strong sense of right and wrong and good and evil, and preservation of tradition. It emphasizes family, respect for authority, and loyalty to the group. It is best seen in traditional religions, the military, conservative politics, patriotism, and country and gospel music.

The modern worldview sees and interprets human life and the world through the lens of reason, science and technology, progress, competition and individual autonomy. It values material wealth, status, education and opportunities. Modern consciousness is dominant in business, science, the mainstream media and sports.

The postmodern worldview sees and interprets reality though the lens of critique of reason and modern consciousness, care for the oppressed and the nature, egalitarianism, multiculturalism and holism. It values the feminine, sensitivity, nature and spirituality. The best examples of postmodern consciousness are seen in academia, especially the humanities, the environmental movement, feminism, the civil rights movement, political correctness movements and the 60's.

The new emerging integral worldview sees human life and the world through the lens of evolution, Spirit, integration of East and West, honoring previous stages, and harmonizing science and religion as well as other fields and perspectives. Since integral consciousness is at the emerging stage we are still awaiting to see how it is going to take shape in the world and its basic values and examples.

The Spirit X vision and teaching honors healthy aspects of each worldview and is deeply inspired by the new emerging integral worldview.

Cultivate critical discernment, my friend. Mind has the capacity to critically evaluate all phenomena including the world, life situations, behaviors, structures and even the self. Healthy and productive criticism is something that is necessary for individual and collective well-being, growth and, indeed, spiritual unfolding and awakening. It has often been the lack of critical mind that lead to much of the abuse and dysfunction in present-day spiritual communities.

Keep yourself—that is, your separate self—psychologically healthy, my friend. We are fortunate to have myriad of psychological teachings and practices available to us today.

# Spirit X

Psychology informs us and helps us with our mind, behavior, unconscious, social interaction, human development, sexuality and even trans-personal domains. In Spirit X, we often talk about psycho-spiritual practices, given the overlap between psychology and spirituality. However, an important distinction has to be made here: while the vast majority of psychological teachings and practices focus on our separate self, the major task of genuine spirituality is to transcend the separate self and realize our True Self. The truth is, it is easier to transcend a healthy separate self than an unhealthy one. And, a psychologically healthy separate self is a better and more productive vehicle for expressing trans-personal and spiritual qualities of Compassion, Wisdom, Peace and Bliss.

Before Enlightenment—psychology, in the name of realizing our True Self. After Enlightenment—psychology, in the name of healthy, clean and polished Service and Expression.

And, alas, the individual mind dissolves and will dissolve completely. The over-identification with the mind leads inevitably to suffering. Thus, like with the body, the practice of the mind for Spirit X practitioners means holding the beautiful paradox of the human condition: I keep my mind open, rich and flexible, in spite of the fact that it dissolves and will dissolve completely. I fully honor my mind by not over-identifying with it.

Mind dissolves... What remains? Be That.

A little exercise: instead of referring to your body and mind as "my body" and "my mind", refer to it as "a mind" and "a body" or "this mind" and "this body". Notice the change. Embody and Be that change.

May you cultivate a healthy, strong and flexible body and an open, rich and flexible mind.

# #14
# Align with Your Relative Purpose and Fulfill Your Absolute Purpose

The relative purpose of your life is the reason you exist in a relative, mind-body form and the absolute purpose of human life is Self-Realization. Aligning with your relative purpose is an important station on your spiritual journey and it leads to fulfilling your absolute, ultimate purpose. Aligning with one's relative purpose is becoming a mainstream phenomenon in the global world, while fulfillment of our ultimate purpose still awaits its full recognition and utilization.

To define and align with your relative life purpose simply ask and live the following questions and inquiries: What is my reason to exist? Why am I here? What is my major contribution to others and the world? What is my unique gift to others and the world? If you want to bring your inquiry to another level and activate some trans-personal juices you can ask: What is my offering to the Divine? How is it to live as an expression of devotion to the Divine?

# Relative Purpose and Absolute Purpose

The key is to live those questions. It is not about the answer, it is about the lived experience. The process of defining and aligning with your life purpose may take some time, so patience and perseverance are sometimes necessary.

A helpful middle step in defining your purpose is defining your core values first. What are the core values you live by? What matters to you most? What do you pay attention to and act on? What are your theoretical and practical principles? Is it spirituality, wellbeing, healing, helping others, justice, duty, compassion, integrity, playfulness? Or environmentalism, feminism, arts, family, political freedom, financial freedom, sports, adventure, etc? Identify your 5-10 core values. After you are in touch with your core values, you can investigate your life purpose.

Life purpose may change during one's lifetime. It often develops in a transcend-and-include fashion with a common thread to it. For instance, in my case, I was first a passionate student of western philosophy, investigating the nature of self and reality, then, I taught philosophy at several universities helping students expand their minds and find meaning of life and, now, I am a full-time spiritual teacher and author helping spiritual practitioners live a spiritual and awakened lives. My life purpose has developed from student to professor to spiritual teacher and it may take some further—and maybe surprising—developments. In that sense, you may define and align with your life purpose for the next 5-10 years or you may define and align with your life purpose for a whole lifetime, still allowing for a possible change and further re-defining and development.

In terms of spiritual growth and unfolding, aligning with your life purpose will connect you with your soul and build a solid station for further growth and unfolding towards being and expressing your True Self. The biggest benefit from aligning with your relative life purpose is that it connects you to and activates something bigger than yourself (as ego). It's an elegant way to transcend the ego.

Other benefits from aligning with your purpose include more enthusiasm, inspiration and meaning, the care for others and the planet, a sense of mission (how your purpose affects others), greater harmony with the world, easy overcoming of obstacles, fearlessness, activation of trans-personal energies, satisfaction that leads to Bliss and devotional service to the Divine.

Take few deep breaths, into the belly and out. Bring forth your sense of purpose and mission. Who are you? How do

# Relative Purpose and Absolute Purpose

you feel? What are others to you? What is the world?

The absolute, ultimate purpose of human life is Self-Realization, re-discovering your True Self, re-membering who and what you really are. Self-Realization in present day society is not an easy task and depends upon effort (practice), grace and karma. It is not enough to understand what Self-Realization is cognitively, the key is taste it experientially, to be it and express it. The best conditions for Self-Realization is to create a Buddha-Dharma-Sangha container. Self-Realization is not the end of ego, but the end of ego-identification.

May you align with your life purpose and fulfill your ultimate purpose. May you help others do the same.

# #15
# CONNECT WITH YOUR SOUL

In Spirit X teaching the spectrum of your True and Full Self is the development and unfolding from ego to soul to the True Self. Connecting with your soul and brining the soul forward as your spiritual center of gravity is a huge step on the spiritual journey. In some wisdom traditions the soul is bypassed (Advaita Vedanta, Zen Buddhism) and in some it is misunderstood (Christianity, Islam). Nevertheless, the movement from identifying with the ego to identifying with the soul is a crucial one.

☉

The soul is a part of your being beyond body and mind, it does not belong to the physical and mental realm and cannot be experienced by the senses, seen or understood. It is also the part of your being that survives physical death—what a relief!

The soul is your last sense of individuality—centered around soul's evolution—and beyond that there is only universal Spirit. The soul completes its evolution by fully merging with pure Spirit. The soul is the last drop of individuality dropping into the ocean of absolute Spirit.

The world of the soul is a subtle world of energy, clairvoyance, clairaudience and clairsentience, illuminations, visions, divine Insight, contemplation of Truth, Beauty and Goodness, spiritual evolution through wisdom and love, communion with subtle archetypes, service to the Divine, etc.

↺

Ego likes to be in the driver's seat of your life and in the spectrum of your True and Full Self; it likes to control, to be in charge, to be always right. The movement from identifying with ego to identifying with the soul consists of bringing the soul forward and giving the soul the opportunity to drive your self and "convincing" the ego to rest a bit in the backseat.

↺

One of the best ways to connect with your soul and to bring it forward is to do the soul inquiry. Simply assume that you have lived, at the soul level, numerous lifetimes, rest in the soul space-time of spiritual evolution and ask yourself and live the following questions: Why did I come back? Why did I reincarnate? What is my unfinished business when it comes to my soul's evolution? What are my unfulfilled noble desires? What more do I need to learn about self, reality and cosmic evolution? What more do I need to give to myself, others, the world and the Divine? What are the issues regarding wisdom and love that I am working on in this lifetime? Finally, what do I need to do to get released from the cycle of birth, death and rebirth and be one with the Source?

# Spirit X

↻

Why did you reincarnate, my friend?

↻

Another superb way to bring your soul forward is to have and live a spiritual vision. The soul simply feeds on vision. Vision here doesn't mean only the vision for your life but also the vision for humanity: the world where we connect deeper, where we bring forth more wisdom and love, where we rely upon evolutionary creativity. What would—in your wildest vision—a more spiritual world look like? What can you do today—or even right now—to make that happen? How can you help others—and indeed, co-create with others—to make that vision reality?

↻

One more way to bring your soul forward is to contemplate Truth, Beauty and Goodness in the physical, mental and spiritual realm of human existence. The teaching of Truth, Beauty and Goodness is an ancient one and is deeply ingrained in our civilization and global culture. With his theory of eternal forms or ideas, ancient Greek philosopher and mystic Plato revealed to us an aspect of the nature of reality that can be utilized on the spiritual path. According to him, the whole manifest reality is nothing but an emanation of the eternal forms of Beauty, Truth and Goodness. Before the soul incarnates into the mind-body and human realm, it contemplates the forms of Beauty, Truth and

Goodness. And when the soul leaves the mind-body and human realm, it goes back to the realm of eternal forms and contemplates pure Beauty, Truth and Goodness.

However, Beauty, Truth and Goodness can also be contemplated in our human realm. And, by doing so, the soul can be re-awaken in this realm and in the mind-body.

What kind of Beauty is appealing to you? What kind of Beauty takes your breath away? Examples in the physical, mental and spiritual realm of human existence include the beauty of the human body and nature, music, literature, paintings and other arts, architecture, mathematical formula or proof, philosophical insight, spiritual vision, recognizing your True Self, etc.

What kind of Truth opens your being and connects you with your core? Examples in the physical, mental and spiritual realm of human existence include honesty and integrity of your partner, family member or a friend; science, humanities, politician's vision, the uncomfortable socio-political truth revealed by whistleblowers, technological breakthroughs of Silicon Valley entrepreneurs, spiritual vision and insight, the ultimate Truth of realizing your True Self, etc.

Finally, what kind of Goodness opens you to a deeper dimension of your being and brings your soul forward? Examples in the physical, mental and spiritual realms of human existence include a mother breastfeeding her child, a stranger helping a homeless person, a family member or a friend offering help right when you need it, a visionary

# Spirit X

politician serving his or her country or humankind, a scientist finding a solution or cure to a major problem, angels, guides and subtle archetypes helping you on your path, Spirit holding this universe and myriad other universes and much more.

If you want to deepen you soul work you can move from contemplating Beauty, Truth and Goodness to embodying and expressing Beauty, Truth and Goodness. How do you bring Beauty to the world? Which kind of activity or creativity makes you share inner our outer Beauty with others? What are you favorite expression of Truth and Goodness and how do they affect others and the world?

Inquire which kind of Beauty, Truth and Goodness brings your soul forward and enjoy the process.

↺

In the subtle world of the soul there are other subtle beings. While connecting with your soul you may encounter subtle guides, angels, saints, deities, gods, goddesses, subtle archetypes, etc. They may offer you guidance or help—and that is considered to be certainly a lucky karmic circumstance. What is called deity yoga has been a major part of many wisdom traditions, especially in Buddhism and Hinduism. Acknowledge Jesus, Krishna, Tara, Kuan Yin, Kali and other subtle beings and expand the space of your spiritual practice and life. Connecting with the subtle world and mastering it is the next collective step in our spiritual and human evolution.

May we all create a more soulful world together. A global soul culture fueled by subtle luminosity, spiritual evolution, deeper lessons in wisdom and love, instead of ego-materialistic driven world.

SPIRIT X

#16

# REALIZE YOUR TRUE SELF

Self-Realization is both an end and a beginning. It is the end of the spiritual journey in that it is the end of seeking as a major mode of one's being. It is also the end of ego-identification. Self-Realization is a new radical beginning, a rebirth of sort, the beginning of a new destiny, a life of service and expression of Spirit, a life in human form that transcends (and includes) the human form.

In many traditions there are a variety of terms for your True Self: Buddha Nature, Christ Consciousness, Atman that is Brahman, the Tao, and many more. The term True Self is chosen carefully in Spirit X for many reasons. True Self does not carry the religious luggage with itself and it points to one's innermost being and intimacy with all things, internally and externally, beyond separation.

One of the most important things regarding the True Self, to understand cognitively and taste spiritually, is that it cannot be discovered, it can be only re-discovered. The

## Realize Your True Self

True Self is not discovered in a sense that the subject discovers the object through the experience. The True Self is re-discovered in a sense that the subject re-laxes and re-leases itself into its own Source beyond all experience, separation and duality. This re-discovery can happen only in the Here and Now and it does not happen in the future. That's why stopping seeking as a major spiritual mode is the key.

Paradoxically, you know your True Self only by being it, or by being That.

Spiritual practices can be divided into seeking practices and presence practices. Seeking practices, like various healing, self-improvement and manifestation practices are future oriented: one day you will achieve your goal, one day you will be healthy, one day you will be happy and whole. (One day, you will be enlightened—oops, it doesn't happen that way). Presence practices stop various kinds of seeking and bring your attention to the Here and Now. Although seeking practices have their place in spirituality, our True Self can be re-discovered only via presence practices.

One of the common mistakes practitioners make regarding the True Self is that they expect to encounter it, to see it with a spiritual eye. They master various techniques, close their eyes, enact spiritual realities and wait to see it like a spiritual object or entity. But the True Self is not there. It

# Spirit X

is not something to be seen, it is the Seer, my friend. That which is aware of body, mind, the world and spiritual realities is your True Self. Rest as the Seer and be the Seer. The only way to know your True Self is to Be the True Self.

That which reads these words is... your True Self.

When you rest as a Seer, the boundary between the Seer, seeing and the seen dissolves into the Godhead.

The realization of the True Self, actually, has two very subtle stages: first, the realization of the Seer, the ever-present Witness of every experience and, second, a release of the Seer itself into seer-seeing-seen, the Godhead.

A tricky aspect of realizing your True Self is that it is literally no-self. It is pure and empty of your small, separate self. And, that absence of the self is, actually, the presence of the Self.

A wonderful aspect of your True Self is that it is all-pervading, it permeates all of Reality. We dive within by resting our attention in the Source, just to re-discover that our most intimate being is all-pervading, already one and intimate with Everything. What a surprise! What a trick! What a relief!

## Realize Your True Self

Pay attention to your body
Notice body sensations coming and going, arising and dissolving
Allow both comfort and discomfort
Notice the instance within you that is aware of body
It is beyond body… but still You.

Pay attention to your mind
Notice the mind activity
Thoughts, images, judgments, interpretations, stories, visions
All coming and going, arising and dissolving
Simply observe your mind without getting wrapped up in it
Notice the instance within you that is aware of the mind
It is beyond the mind… but still You.

Now, get ready for an important turn:
Notice the Noticer
Be aware of Awareness
This is intimately and ultimately You
Be That
Embrace body-mind-world from this placeless place.
Allow even the Noticer to dissolve
Into the Suchness of Being
Divine Godhead.

# Spirit X

Be aware of your thoughts
Distinguish between thoughts and Awareness
Let thoughts come and go
By being aware of thoughts you are free from thoughts.

Be aware of your personality
Notice what you think, feel, prefer and avoid
Right now and moment-to-moment
By being aware of your personality you are free from your personality.

Be aware of space-time
As basic categories of the whole manifest world
Notice "here" and notice "there"
Notice "now" and notice "then"
By being aware of space-time you are free from space-time.

Be aware of Awareness
Be That which has been aware since you have known yourself
And before that
By being aware of Awareness you are what your truly are
Include the body-mind-world into your most intimate Self
Simply Be
Freely and Fully.

You are Awareness experiencing Itself
In its eternal and infinite Display.

# Realize Your True Self

Look into your child's eyes—the Self.
Look into your lover's eyes—the Self.
Look into a stranger's eyes—the Self.
Look at a flower—the Self.
Look at the sky—the Self.
Look at a dog's poop—the Self.
Look at myriad universes beyond this one—the Self.
Within and without—the Self.

An important moment and stage on the spiritual journey —that relates a great deal to Self-Realization—is to see-through and feel-through the paradox of seeking. Awakening is about realizing That which you already are but are overlooking. Seeking simply does not reveal to you that which you already are, your True Self. As human beings we are evolutionarily wired to seek, strive and desire. And it is so easy to behave that way on our spiritual journey, too. The paradox of seeking consists in the fact that you are seeking something that you already are; you are desiring something that you already have. Once this paradox is seen-though and felt-through one surrenders to the Here and Now beyond egoic picking and choosing. Surrender is the last step on the spiritual journey and the most advanced spiritual practice in that sense.

# Spirit X

Surrender, my friend, and gently fall into your True Self.

Whether awake or asleep
Whether happy or sad
Whether man or woman
Your True Self is there for you
In the Here and Now
Like the most faithful Friend
Waiting to be re-discovered.

A hint of Integral Yoga: Hug your True Self.

Gently close your eyes
Take few deep breaths
Into the belly
And out
Into the belly
And out
Notice how close to you is your breath
Your True Self is closer to you than your breath
It is so close to you
That there is no distance
Between you and That.

# Realize Your True Self

Whether one has an initial awakening (glimpse of True Self with further coming and going of it) or abiding awakening (stable awakening at all times) is not the key issue here. The key is to at least glimpse your True Self. All you need is a glimpse. That glimpse will, little by little, permeate your mind-body, inform everything you do and stabilize itself as a center of your being. At this point of evolution, there is no need to mystify awakening and reserve it for only a few chosen ones. Spirit needs you, Evolution needs you, Life needs you and you need That. And all you need is a glimpse.

So, what is the promise of Self-Realization? How does one's life unfolds after awakening? What is enlightened living like? Realization and expression are two sides of the same coin. After awakening, one by definition aligns with the noble desire to help others re-discover their True Self. That expression and that service can certainly take many unique flavors, it can be dynamic or static, it can be private or public, it may be in spiritual, healing, or social arena—but nonetheless, one cannot help but to help others have the same realization. Another feature of enlightened living is that it is not ego-centered and that may influence many areas of your life such as relationships, family, sex, work, career, and creativity. Enlightened life is the life of ease, flow, non-resistance to what is and indeed, a life of fearlessness and fierceness when necessary. It is a life with more energy, enthusiasm and creative power.

# Spirit X

Human life is often seen like a movement from birth to death and, if we are lucky and work on it, it is filled with purpose, value and meaning. From a a spiritual perspective, human life is a movement from birth to Self-Realization. We come to this dimension to taste Liberation in its full spectrum, to continue the search or even to complete it. Acknowledging that cognitively and utilizing it spiritually is the single best thing one can do in one's life. The consequences of this approach are literally unimaginable to the mind.

Look, my friend, at the world around you
Look at the world within you
And first and foremost
Look at the... Looker.

Prior to your personality
Prior to your parents
Prior to Jesus and Buddha
Prior to the Big Bang
You are your True Self.

May you realize your True Self and help others do the same.

# #17
# Death Is a Transition

If done properly, spiritual unfolding radically changes our relationship to death in a relieving and liberating way. The truth is, death is our surest possibility. In the human condition, we may do this or that, or become this or that, or achieve this or that, but the sure thing is that we will all die one day. Egoic consciousness has a twofold—and not that productive—relationship to death: it fears it and represses it. In that way, death becomes something that limits and ends our life, something that we don't want to consider, and after which we have no idea what to expect. Death is a combination of a pressing limit, end, fear, repression and uncomfortable unknown. However, the wisdom within the spectrum of our True and Full Self is: ego dies, soul survives death and lives numerous lifetimes in everlasting soul space-time, and the True Self is absolutely beyond the cycle of birth, death and rebirth. Ego is just a small part within the spectrum of your True and Full Self.

Death puts pressure on ego and makes one's time short, one's space tight and one's decisions ignorant. Soul exists lifetime after lifetime in the everlasting spiritual evolution of lessons in wisdom and love. The True Self is beyond existence in the timeless Now. Ego dies, soul is immortal, the True Self is timeless.

# Spirit X

Releasing the fear and pressure of death and dropping into the deeper dimension of our being is key not only for individual and collective spiritual evolution but for individual and collective sanity and well-being at this challenging and inspiring point of human evolution.

†•

The spiritual response to the death issue is that you die before you die. You die to ego-identification before you die physically. Spiritual growth and unfolding means that you move the center of gravity of your spiritual identity from ego to soul to True Self. And, the end of ego-identification radically transform our relationship to death.

†•

"Die before dying" we hear often across wisdom traditions. It basically means: practice and transcend—and include—your ego.

†•

Death is not opposite to life, it is opposite to birth. From a spiritual perspective, it is easy to notice that, actually, death is a part of the fabric of Life.

Look at the sleep cycle. In the waking state, we identify with the gross mind-body strongly separated from the world, while dreaming we have a dream mind-body (no physical body in the subtle-mind world) and, in deep dreamless sleep there is neither mind-body nor the world, only pregnant Void, Nirvana. So in terms of our states of consciousness, death is a part of the fabric of human condition.

Or, look at the meditation practice. If done properly, every time you sit on the cushion, you drop the mind-body and die. So dying—as ego-transcendence—is an inherent part of every genuine spiritual practice.

And, the list is long. When you do what you love, you die to that activity. When you orgasm, you die to the Bliss of Being. When you contemplate Beauty, you die to it... Lots of dying before physical dying within the fabric of Life.

†•

Can you die to your ego, right Here, right Now, my friend?

†•

The spiritual journey as a process is mostly a pleasurable and fun affair with some stages where we need to do dirty, uncomfortable work and face some demons (letting go of or transforming habits, shadow work, dark night of the soul, etc). However, some stages of the spiritual journey may feel like a physical death, when our internal or external circumstances shift and the new frequency hasn't picked up fully. Those stages may be accompanied with unease, fear, confusion and a sense of being lost on the path, loss of the self and, indeed, of dying. In those moments, the best approach is not to panic, still trust the process and

# Spirit X

rely on your Buddha-Dharma-Sangha spiritual container. Those are the moments when we are grateful that we are not alone on the path.

† •

Science, technology, spirituality and other fields of human activity are working on giving us answers and, more importantly, evidence of what happens to us when we die. That will certainly change the way we live. In the meantime, we can all try to release the fear around death, recognize it as a transition and die before we die. As Zen master put it, death is just taking off the coat of mind-body.

Know cognitively and realize experientially: ego dies, soul lives forever, True Self is timeless.

# Part II
# The World

# Spirit X

# #18
# LIKE SPIRIT, REALITY HAS TWO DIMENSIONS: UNMANIFEST AND MANIFEST

The purpose of the Part 2 is to utilize the world for our spiritual growth and unfolding. By world, we mean here the totality of both inner and outer phenomena revealed to the practitioner. The desk is real in physical reality, a thought is real in mental reality, Krishna is real in spiritual reality. In what follows we will mostly explore how conventional reality can be utilized on our spiritual journey.

There are, indeed, many ways to approach and interpret reality. Like with our approach to Spirit, the best way to approach reality from a spiritual perspective, is to acknowledge cognitively and recognize spiritually that there are two dimensions of reality: ultimate and relative, unmanifest and manifest. Unmanifest reality is an empty screen upon which myriad universes arise, shine and dissolve (including your little ego) and relative reality is the world as all outer and inner phenomena and forms. Unmanifest reality is pure consciousness, manifest reality is consciousness as forms and phenomena. Mastering both dimensions of reality—as well

## Spirit X

as their not-twoness—is of crucial importance in Spirit X teaching.

#19

# Manifest Reality Is Multidimensional and a Spectrum

The most distinctive feature of relative, manifest reality from a spiritual standpoint is that it is multidimensional. There is the reality or worldspace of the body, the reality of the mind, the reality of the spirit, there is virtual reality, there are inner forms, outer forms, there are individual phenomena, there are collectives. Part of spiritual training and a big part of spiritual practice includes being aware of and mastering various dimensions of relative reality. If you want a healthy body, that requires acknowledging the body-worldspace and mastering it to an extent. The same with relationships, building a successful business or yearning for spiritual awakening.

The world is rich, so are you, as your attention moves through various dimensions of reality. Enjoy the surf.

Another distinctive feature of manifest reality is that it is a

# Spirit X

spectrum, a movement from matter to life to mind to soul to Spirit. This evolutionary insight into the evolutionary fabric of relative reality is of crucial importance for present day spirituality. Through that lens and via that cosmic feature, the cosmos is seen, revealed and activated like a movement from matter to Spirit; human life is a movement from birth to Self-Realization; human history is progress towards an enlightened world. All of a sudden there are stairways to Heaven everywhere.

# #20
# Unmanifest Reality Is Beyond Space and Time, and Beyond the Cycle of Birth, Death and Rebirth

The biggest legacy and blessing from the world wisdom traditions—Christianity, Hinduism, Buddhism, Islam, Taoism—is the pointing to and realization of your True Self, which is absolute consciousness, ultimate Reality, the not-two of manifest and unmanifest Reality. The realization of and access to the unmanifest domain of Reality is crucial for Awakening, Liberation and a genuine spiritual life in general. As long as we are only in the domain of manifest reality—relational, social or virtual; gross, subtle or causal—various kinds of bondage and suffering can occur. Real Liberation lies beyond body-mind-world. And thank God for the wisdom traditions and their ultimate gift to us.

The unmanifest and ultimate aspects of Reality have to be realized spiritually; however, knowing that possibility cognitively as our highest potential is equally important. In healthy cultures and societies, cognition precedes realization, first we know about our highest potential, Atman that is Brahman, the oneness of our essence and the essence of Reality—and then we realize it.

Inquire wholeheartedly: What is really real? Discriminate between that which is permanent and that which is transient. Only that which is permanent is really real.

Samsara in wisdom traditions is the cycle of suffering, that is, the cycle of birth, death and rebirth. You incarnate into the human realm—or other realms—you live and love, do some spiritual work and good deeds, you die, you come back and continue to live and do spiritual work and good deeds, you die again, you are born again… and again… and again. Such is the cycle of suffering. One fully completes the journey when one fully realizes the nature of Reality and offers good deeds in accordance with it. And there is no full realization without realizing unmanifest and ultimate dimensions of Reality. Which is identical to your True Self.

The Sanskrit word "Dharma" has many meanings, the nature of reality, teaching, absolute truth, the teaching of Buddhism, cosmic law and order, duty. Perhaps the best meaning in the context of contemporary spirituality would be that Dharma is the teaching that reveals Reality, both relative and ultimate, both manifested and unmanifested and shapes human life in accordance to it.

The sciences, psychology, humanities and other teachings regarding manifest reality help us to understand and navigate the manifest realm, bring value, purpose, meaning and healing to human life and dimension, deliver certain degree of emancipation—but they cannot liberate us fully. Only teachings that point to and reveal the ultimate and unmanifest in us and Reality can deliver full Realization and Liberation. And that's why, ultimately, we are here in the human dimension.

What is permanent in waking, dreaming and deep dreamless sleep? What is permanent in the cycle of night and day? What is permanent in cosmic and human evolution? What is permanent in birth, death and rebirth? What is in the gap between your two thoughts?

Beyond and
Beyond
Is
Ultimate Reality
Manifest and Unmanifest
As not-two
Your True Self.

Spirit X

#21

# The World Is the Place to Make an Effort Towards Ego-Transcendence, Wisdom and Love, and Self-Realization

Whether you are interested in ego-transcendence, or cultivating your soul (by bringing it forward) via wisdom and love, or in Self-Realization, the world is the place to do it. Whether you aspire more peace for yourself, or a better world, or a great spiritual life, or a favorable rebirth, or total liberation, or to be a new Buddha or Jesus, the world is the place to do it. From a spiritual standpoint, the world is the widest possible container for our spiritual growth and unfolding. From an ultimate perspective, the world—and every little piece of it—is nothing but the immediate portal to our Liberation and Self-Realization.

As much as practice and effort are important (for attaining wisdom), service and good deeds (expression of love), are equally important. The best thing to do is to incorporate practice and service together at the very start of your spiritual life. And the world is the place to do it. Engagement with others and the word is the opportunity for your—and everybody's—growth and, even, Awakening.

Instead of turning the world into an obstacle on the path —full of negative and positive attachments, picking and choosing—use the world for ego-transcendence, cultivation of the soul through wisdom and love and Self-Realization. The world is the place to show effort, and practice and serve.

SPIRIT X

## #22
# CONNECT WITH OTHERS

Humans are both highly autonomous and communal beings. There is no happy, successful and enlightened life without a healthy balance of autonomy and communion. While solitude, withdrawal from the world and autonomy —especially in a monastic setting—have been the major mode in spirituality for centuries, today we are experiencing the emergence of spirituality which is more relational and engaged with the world. The truth is: we are in this together. We are all a bit lost, thrown into this mysterious game called Life, and we are all helping each other to find the way Home.

Without Sangha—a group of fellow spiritual practitioners —spiritual growth is difficult, if not impossible. Together with the Buddha and the Dharma, Sangha constitutes the right three-leg container for spiritual practice and growth. Other practitioners help us heal, transform and, indeed, enlighten. They point out our blind spots and empower us on the spiritual journey.

Spend high quality time with your Sangha. Identify how

you benefit from it, what is your offering to the Sangha and be deeply grateful for it. Once you have got comfortable with your Sangha—extend it in concentric circles; include your family, coworkers, neighbors, fellow-citizens until you include all sentient being in it. You can even include non-sentient phenomena in your Sangha.

May you find a Sangha, wherever you are.

The human condition is integrally rich in terms of human interaction.

Connect with others physically: exercise together, play sports, have sex with your partner, do yoga with your Sangha, dance, hike—in a word, sweat meaningfully with others.

Connect with others emotionally: share with others your feelings and emotions and receive others on that level.

Connect with others mentally: share and exchange ideas, engage in intellectual debates, create resonance on the mental level.

Connect with others spiritually: meditate together, practice all other forms of spirituality together, share silence together.

# Spirit X

Participate in the we-space of culture: create and attend events in which you resonate deeply with others.

Participate in the we-space of society: engage socially, politically, environmentally, etc.

❊

This integral richness of human interaction will open your being and be a great ally on your journey of re-discovery of your True Self.

❊

Look at the eyes of your partner, child, friend or a stranger. Stay there for a while. What do you See?

❊

On an ultimate level—there are no others. Yet we realize that by the vehicle of genuine connection with others.

❊

May others release you into your True Self.
May you release others into their True Self.

#23

# Commune with Nature

For German idealist and integral philosopher Hegel, nature is nothing but externalization of the Absolute Idea. In terms of the spectrum of cosmic consciousness in this universe—from matter to life to mind to soul to Spirit—nature is a level in itself, and a station without which other levels of consciousness cannot emerge. No nature, no mind. No nature, no human beings. We live in times of serious reconsideration of our relationship to nature and that is certainly of great significance to the role of nature in our spiritual growth and unfolding.

From a spiritual perspective, nature is—alongside with Sangha—a superb container for our spiritual practice and life. Spending time in nature has many benefits for our health as well as for spiritual life. Now more than ever humans have access to various types of nature on a global level and it is time to utilize that spiritually to the fullest extent.

Make communing with nature regular. Do it on your own

or with others. Be honest and clear with yourself in determining which type of nature works best for you. Is it mountains? Is it ocean? Is is desert? Notice what happens to your mind-body when you commune with your favorite type of nature. Notice how communing with nature affects your relationship with others and with life in general. What can you learn from nature?

An important aspect of communing with nature is that the beauty of nature can produce major spiritual openings. Cultivate states of Awe in nature. Simply allow the beauty of nature to fully take your attention, stop your mind, blow you away and open your entire being.

The sound of birds singing in the morning.
Awe.
Gentle breeze felt on your skin.
Awe.
Fool moon on a clear night.
Awe.
A horizon, where ocean meets the sky.
Awe.
Sitting on a bench in the city park.
Awe.
A hike in the national park.
Awe.
Lauterbrunnen Valley in the Swiss Alps on a clear day.

# Commune with Nature

Awe.
The orange glory of the Grand Canyon.
Awe.
Presence of Shiva in the Mount Kailash.
Yogic Stillness and Power.
Beyond Awe.
The Babaji feel in the Himalayas. The descent of an Avatar.
Beyond Awe.

Contemplate the desert. Or a mountain. Notice how it feels as though it may have been there for a long time, much longer than an average human life, perhaps longer than civilization itself. A desert or a mountain have been there for almost forever. Rest your mind in that "almost forever" time and feel. Rest your mind in forever time and feel. Finally, rest your mind beyond time.

We live in challenging environmental times. As a consequence of global industrialization, we started using nature as a mere resource and created economic and environmental habits that are threatening the life of the planet and the life of our species. It is time to reconsider both cognitively and spiritually our relationship to nature and planet Earth. Cognitively, we can rethink what nature is—for our mind indeed—and our relationship to it. Spiritually, we can appreciate and connect with nature more. Realizing and approaching nature as Spirit and a station in the spectrum of cosmic

# Spirit X

evolution can certainly heal and transform the problematic habits we have created related to nature and planet Earth.

♣

Look at the planet Earth. Isn't she beautiful? Envision in your mind's eye our planet as the cosmic ornament of Spirit—something that our planet already is and has the potential to become even more so. Envision people, culture, technology and other human activities consciously working to turn Earth into an expression of the perfection of Spirit. Envision beings from other galaxies and dimensions contemplating Earth and being deeply moved and inspired by its beauty and spiritual radiance.

♣

Planet Earth. Awe.

♣

Be still like a Mountain.
Flow like a River.
Be ancient like a Desert.
Be vast like an Ocean.
Be open like the Sky.

♣

May we make Earth our true and full Home,
A radiant ornament of Spirit.

#24

# Relationships and Sex Are Means for Spiritual Growth and Unfolding

The vast majority of present day spiritual practitioners are in some sort of relationship with others: romantic, family, professional, visionary, spiritual, etc. In the new emerging global spirituality that is genuinely engaged with the world rather than ascetic towards it, relationships are an important and unavoidable module. And indeed, that module can be transformed into a vehicle of transformation and awakening.

☯

Just like Sangha (spiritual community) and nature, romantic relationships can be turned into powerful containers for spiritual growth and unfolding. If in a relationship, commit to growing-up together and relaxing together. The growing-up together spiritual module refers to practices and activities that open your mind and heart to more depth, complexity, wider-and-wider perspectives, compassion, and deeper connectivity. When was the last time you attended a workshop together with your partner? Or did some psychological or healing work? Or traveled, experienced and navigated foreign lands together? Growing-up together will make sure that you and your partner are growing together into a better and better version of You.

The re-lax spiritual module refers to radically slowing down the karma of body-mind-world and staying simply present with your partner. When was the last time you and your partner shared silence together? Or meditated together? Or had a day without an agenda? Or spent few days off the grid? Re-laxing together can open you and your partner to unimaginable insight, depth and connection.

Make sure that you and your partner stay in touch with various levels of your relationship: physical, emotional, mental and spiritual.

Couples who sweat together—stay together. Sweating can take the shape of exercising, dancing, hiking, having sex, etc.

Couples who exchange emotions—stay together. Make sure that healthy giving and receiving of emotions is present in your relationship.

Couples who think together—stay together. Thinking together can take shape of reading together, discussion, attending lectures, learning foreign languages, developing mindset and worldview, etc.

Couples who practice spirituality together—stay together. Practicing spirituality together can take shape of meditating, doing yoga, attending workshops and retreats, hanging out with the Sangha, etc.

Sexuality is one of the strongest forces in the human realm. Whether for reproduction and continuation of our species or for shallow and deep pleasure—sexuality is not something to be overlooked and something to be utilized for spiritual growth and unfolding. In wisdom traditions we find opposite attitudes and prescriptions regarding sexuality: from overcoming and repression in ascetic traditions to the full acknowledgment and utilization in tantric traditions. The truth is, depending on one's spiritual typology, sex can be a powerful tool for transformation and awakening.

From fucking, to making love, to sacred sexuality—human sexuality provides ways we intimately connect with each other and taste levels of connectedness and Reality.

Fuck your babe—feel the pleasure of sex on a basic level.

Make love to your babe—include the deeper dimension of your being—love, respect, mutual humanity—into your sexuality.

Engage in sacred sexuality with your babe—approach your

# Spirit X

partner as the Divine who will take you to the Ultimate.

Merge with your partner and re-lax into your togetherness. What is the ultimate glue that brings you and keeps you together?

Merge with your partner and re-lax into your beingness. Where did you go when you merged together?

For Her: Open your being to your partner—and the world—play and dance together and re-lax.

For Him: Penetrate your partner—and the world—play and dance together and re-lax.

If your relationship culminates into a family, you are blessed. A woman, a man, a child or children—what a holy container for spiritual growth and unfolding. Not without its challenges and hardships, family throughout human evolution has always stood and will stand as the foundation of spiritual life. In family as a spiritual container, we balance the duties and responsibilities of everyday life with genuine spiritual practice. If you are a family person, the key is introducing spiritual practices, rituals and games into your family life as early as possible.

For Her: Take your babe by the hand and take him Home, physically, sexually, emotionally, mentally and spiritually.

For Him: Take your babe by the hand and take her Home, physically, sexually, emotionally, mentally and spiritually.

## #25
# Work, Career and Money Are Means for Spiritual Growth and Unfolding

Although, in global culture and economy, we are considering other options to work, career and money such as universal basic income, automation, the gig economy, bitcoin, and other options, work, career and money will likely be an important part of our everyday lives and conventional reality for a while. In the meantime, whatever the outcome is, we can turn them into the vehicles of spiritual growth and unfolding.

🧍 $ 🧍

First things first: work, career and money have been too often considered to be obstacles on the path, rather than essential part of it and an opportunity on the path. This kind of view and belief system does not help in present day global spirituality. Everything—including work, career and money—can be turned into the vehicles of transformation and awakening. Thus, simply start there: work, career and

## Work, Career and Money

money are part of your spiritual practice as much as meditation, satsang and tantric sex. Once this mindset about it is changed you can expect the real transformation within that realm of your life to start occurring.

⁂

By work nowadays we mean work for a living. In today's global world, economy is a major force and it cannot be overlooked and ignored. The vast majority of people in today's world have to earn for a living. The daily cycle for most of us consists of 8 hours of work, 8 hours of leisure time and 8 hours of sleep. The key from a spiritual standpoint is to turn those 8 hours of work into a genuine spiritual practice that serves you and others.

⁂

However, the notion of work can be expanded in a spectrum-like fashion. There is manual work, emotional work, mental work, work for a living, visionary work, spiritual work and many other types of work. Like with other spectrum-like maps and realities, the imperative is to move through the spectrum. Don't allow your work for a living to be the only kind of work you do.

⁂

In the age of the emergence of cyber and virtual spaces, which are mind-oriented and exclude the body, the key is to still engage in manual labor. Clean your house and yard, do the laundry, make some food, help others move and arrange their homes, chop wood and carry water as they say in Zen—all of those activities put you in a genuine contact with your environment on a manual and physical level. You have a body, you have a mind and you are essentially Spirit. We are holistic, integral and multidimensional beings, and manual labor is always a good reminder and practice of it. For that reason, in Spirit X we strongly recommend regular manual labor as a part of practice and life.

⁑ $ ⁑

As for your work for a living—from a spiritual standpoint, the key is to transform your relationship with it by bringing a higher, divine frequency to it. Work is simply a beautiful way to serve others, our communities and the world as a whole. Work is the offering of your gifts. And we often forget about that. Re-member the divine frequency of your daily job.

⁑ $ ⁑

What is divine about what you do for a living? What is it about it that serves others? What is it about it that serves the preservation, transformation and growth of consciousness? Every profession has a divine spark to it. If you are a janitor, you maintain space for others to work, live and grow. Amen. If you are a professor you expand other people's minds and polish their skills so they can serve others. Amen. If you are a lawyer, you serve justice. Amen. Those divine sparks of what you do for a living can be turned into powerful practices and techniques and can radically transform your life and the life of others.

🕴 $ 🕴

Whatever you do for a living—Amen.

🕴 $ 🕴

Transforming your relationship with what you do for a living may lead you to loving your job more, changing your job, creating your own job, creating jobs for others, the whole process may have its ups and downs—so inherent to the human condition and dimension—but one thing is certain: by transforming your relationship to your daily job, you are doing a huge spiritual favor to yourself, others and the world. For the vast majority of people at this point in human evolution, work represents a point of egoic resistance—and that doesn't help anyone. Transcend (and include) your ego by transforming your relationship to work—an act of engaged in-the-world-out-of-this-world spirituality.

🕴 $ 🕴

By career nowadays we mean a profession done for a longer period of time and accompanied with a sense of progress. The sense of progress usually includes financial and social aspects of one's life. Lately, we are witnessing the expansion of the sense of progress to include other aspects of

# Spirit X

one's life—such as emotional, psychological and spiritual growth—and even progress of other people. From a spiritual standpoint the biggest trick regarding a career is to engage in it without allowing it to hijack your identity and your sense of self. The vast majority of people nowadays over-identify with their profession and career and consider it central of their identity and fulfillment. I am a lawyer, that is who I am, that is how I see the world, and that is what informs my actions. And, if I just continue to progress in it—that is where fulfillment is. Or, I am a coach, that is who I am, that is how I see the world, that is what ultimately informs my actions and that is where fulfillment is. Or, I am an activist, and that is where my identity and fulfillment are.

§ $ §

You know it, my friend: ultimate fulfillment is not in a profession and career. Although, having a successful career may serve your re-discovery of ultimate fulfillment a great deal.

§ $ §

Street cleaners, janitors, teachers, athletes, CEOs, presidents of the countries, pimps and whores—you are all much more than your profession and career. God bless you for what you do—as long as you do it mindfully, skillfully and with integrity. And God bless You—you are much more than that.

# Work, Career and Money

† $ †

Reducing career to only financial and social aspects won't take you far on the spiritual path. Instead, ask yourself how you and others can grow through your career financially, socially, emotionally, psychologically, spiritually, etc.

† $ †

Like ego, money got a bad reputation in spirituality and there is quite a bit of confusion about it. The fact is that money has hijacked a lot of people's minds and hearts and made them do ignorant stuff to themselves, others and the world. But the bigger fact is: money as energy can be mastered, transformed and used from higher perspective and for higher purposes.

† $ †

Money, sex, power—the three energies that ego is so attracted to and the three energies that ego has so much problems handling mindfully, skillfully and with integrity. In the emerging global spirituality it is imperative to approach these three energies from a trans-egoic perspective and to transform our relationship to it.

† $ †

If your life is primarily about making money and there's never enough of it—you are wrapped up in it. If you are in scarce of not having enough money—you are wrapped up in it. If you are rejecting money—like many spiritual practitioners nowadays do—you are still wrapped up in it, this time as a rejection mode. It takes a tremendous amount of energy to negate something and to push it away from your life and consciousness.

† $ †

What is money from a spiritual standpoint? It is a form of energy and a form of abundance that flows among human beings via giving and receiving on several levels—physical, economic, mental—of our mutual existence. Another aspect of money is that it is inherently practical, it simply makes things happen. Money can be used for the transformation of consciousness. And, alas, at this point in human evolution, we won't be able to transform consciousness without money.

† $ †

Imagine you have 1 million dollars. How does it feel? What would you do with it? How would you improve your life and the life of others with it? How would you improve life on Earth with it? How would you improve Spirit on Earth with it?

† $ †

And, alas, work, career and money are often overemphasized, we spend way too much time and energy getting wrapped up in it, so many people can't even see any other aspects of reality, economy as a perspective has been overrated. The trick is to do work, career and money by not getting wrapped up in it. Be in this world by not being of this world. You are Spirit in human form.

## #26
# Culture and Pop-Culture Are Means for Spiritual Growth and Unfolding

Isn't it incredible that in the human condition we can share ideas, meanings and values, that we can connect on that basis and that we can expand that Connection to the point where there is no separation between "me" and "you."

For the purposes of this book and teaching, we define culture as shared values, ideas and acts that create a connection, bond and growth between a group of people that is worthy of preserving and passing on to the next generation. Culture in the human dimension can occur on many levels, from family to region to nation to sub-culture to global and even to cosmic. On a deeper level, culture is a way certain group of people grow together and interpret reality.

# Culture and Pop-Culture

The word culture is derived from the Latin word *cultura* which means cultivation, education and development. So, in the very origin of the word we find the idea that culture is a container for collective growth and development.

Cultural identity can be one of the key factors in maintaining ego-identification (and the continuation of suffering). I am German, this is who we are, this is how we do things, and this is what reality is for us. Or, I am a heavy metal fan and that fully informs the way I see reality and how I act. However, in our global village, culture can be used as a stepping stone to ego-transcendence. By acknowledging that there are other cultures and by implementing some values and practices from them, one's cultural identity becomes wider and more fluid and this makes one's ego wider and more fluid. Wideness and fluidity of the ego eventually lead to the re-discovery of the deeper dimension of our being and our True Self.

Due to the information technology revolution, in the present day global culture, for the first time in human history, we have available to us virtually all the wisdom and information from all the spiritual traditions that ever existed on this planet. Christian, Hindu, Buddhist, Muslim, Taoist and all the other texts, teachings and practices are fully available to the present day spiritual practitioner. That is something not to be underestimated and to be deeply grateful for. In terms of availability of resources—there has never been a better time to be a spiritual practitioner. Lucky you! Lucky us!

Deep Bow to the present day moment in global culture. We have came a long way.

In the present day world, many people derive values, ideas and practices from pop-culture. For the purposes of this book and teaching, we define pop-culture as a set of contents, ideas and practices transmitted via mass media, social media and the Internet that inform people's lives and create a connection between them. Examples of pop-culture include movies, music, TV, video games, sports, fashion, and more. Although often seen as shallow and superficial, pop-culture can be a doorway for deeper investigation of the human condition.

Think of movies, they entertain us, scare us, confuse us, bore us, and, indeed, change our lives. Good movies open our minds and our hearts and propel us into deeper inquiry about the Mystery of existence.

Have you seen *Deer Hunter*, a timeless tale of war and true friendship? With incredible Robert de Niro, Christopher

## Culture and Pop-Culture

Walken and Meryl Streep in it?

Have you seen *Wall Street* and its warning about human greed?

Have you seen *Mulholland Drive* and the way it deconstructs the conventional notions of plot and character and aesthetically portrays Beauty and Mystery?

Have you seen the *Wizard of Oz* and its message that True Home is always right under your feet?

And, have you seen the *Apocalypse Now?*

And then, there is music. After a challenging day, you crank up your favorite song and everything is okay. Fundamentally okay. You drive in your car listening to a beautiful tune and there it is, a peak experience of higher unity and meaning. A timeless tale of the importance and impact of music in the human dimension.

Music—where and when the ordinary and extraordinary come together.

Remember the Monkees: innocence, sweetness, entertainment, fun, great tunes, connecting people all over the globe —pop-culture at its beginning and at its best. Sing with me: *Daydream Believer*

*With or Without You, Love Will Tear Us Apart, You Are Always on My Mind, One Love...* Vibrations of pop-rock music keep shaping, informing and guiding our lives.

*Let It Be* sing and teach The Beatles.

Remember Woodstock and 1969? We were all there.

The two things about pop-culture that make it important and can be utilized on a spiritual path: pop-culture happens through the medium of fun and pop-culture happens on a mass scale. Isn't it great to connect to other human beings based on fun. So, spiritually, let's have profound fun, a playful investigation and journey into the depths of our being and Reality. And isn't it great that pop-culture connects and informs billions of people. Let's make spirituality fun and dive deeper on a large scale.

# Culture and Pop-Culture

*Deeper and Deeper* provokes Madonna, the Queen of Pop.

*Enjoy the Silence* by Depeche Mode invites us to go beyond Sound and Music.

#27

# Art Is a Means for Spiritual Growth and Unfolding

We are blessed to have art in the human condition. Art can heal, teach, uplift, connect us with others and the world and, indeed, enlighten. We are yet to discover the real potential of art in the human world. Aesthetic experience, both a state of appreciation of art and Beauty, and a state of creativity in general, is very close to a spiritual experience, a direct experience of Spirit on multiple levels of Being.

"We have art in order not to perish from the Truth," said German philosopher Nietzsche. The truth Nietzsche refers to here is the truth of Becoming—the fact that Life grows and shrinks, that change is inevitable, at times for better and at times for worse—not the truth of Being which reveals to us Peace, Unity and Bliss. Yet Nietzsche is right—art has such an important existential and therapeutic role in the human universe. We live in times when the real potential of art is yet to be discovered and utilized for human growth and even spiritual enlightenment.

# Art Is a Means for Spiritual Growth

✍

Beauty, Truth and Goodness—the three Platonic ideas as the seeds of the whole manifest realm. And art, science and morals—the three noble human activities that connect our humanity with our Divinity. As it is easy to notice, these three activities are not equally represented in our present day world, that is dominated by science and its methods, worldview and materialism. In that respect, we need arts nowadays more than ever. We also need creativity to rethink and recreate who we are and what is our relationship to others, the world and the Divine.

✍

The spiritual significance of art lies in the fact that aesthetic appreciation of art and Beauty and creativity in general are superb spiritual practices and life-attitudes in general. Aesthetic appreciation of arts and Beauty is a high form of contemplation and a gentle yet sure way of ego-transcendence. Creativity in the arts and life in general is inherent to the human condition, and in this historical moment we have almost no other way but to re-invent ourselves on this planet and in the universe. Not to mention that human creativity connects us with cosmic creativity, the all-powerful Shakti, the divine creative energy of the universe.

✍

Do you have any interest in art? Does art affect you? If so, you are blessed. What is your favorite art and how does inform you and open you? Make sure you expose yourself to art, just the way you make sure you spend some time communing with nature. Make art a habitat for your spiritual growth and unfolding.

---

Are you open to creativity? What are the areas of human life where your creativity shines? Do you like crafts, or building things, or playing music, or writing, or hacking systems and inventing new ones? Cultivate your creativity, you need it and the world needs it. Every act of creativity is a good deed and has a spiritual significance.

---

Art is a state of being: you and the divine Shakti co-creating. Amen.

---

Art is a state of being: appreciation, wonder, creativity, inspiration, flow, spontaneity, Beauty. Who doesn't want those in their lives, others and the world.

---

A hint of integral yoga:
Make your life a work of art
Help others make their lives a work of art
Make the Earth a work of art.

#28

# Utilize Science for Spiritual Growth and Unfolding

By utilizing here we mean a practical application which is a blend of deep appreciation, and cognitive and spiritual discernment. From a spiritual standpoint, science can bee seen as a beautiful paradox: on the one hand, there is deep gratitude for science and for what it has given us; on the other hand, it is clear that science alone won't save us. Thank God for science yet it won't save us. Only scientific progress coupled and balanced with psycho-spiritual, cultural and social growth will save us.

Science, its method, and practical applications in the name of improving our life on this planet, is something to be grateful for and to utilize even further for human well-being, transformation and even awakening. However, science as a worldview fails to recognize the cosmic evolutionary spectrum of consciousness—from matter to life to mind to soul to spirit—and acknowledges only matter and derives the rest of reality from it. Even mind and consciousness are seen as a result of material processes. Thus science overemphasizes the objective dimension of the universe and becomes materialistic both in theory and practice. Scientific materialism, "matter is ultimate", coupled with spiritual materialism, "my ego is the ultimate self"—welcome to the modern world void of depth, deeper meaning and Spirit.

Close your eyes, my friend
Take a few deep breaths
Into the belly
And out
Re-lax
And tell me:
What is ultimately real?

From a spiritual standpoint, the scientific revolution that occurred from 1550 to 1700, had a major spiritual impact. Interpreting reality through the scientific lens and improving our lives by applying it practically on human world and nature made us feel more at home on this planet. The world was governed by laws of nature and not by a judging and punishing God. And those laws of nature can be understood by the human mind—what a major collective relief. The scientific revolution softened the duality between humankind and the world and made us more at home in the world. However, by doing that, it overemphasized reason and empirical knowledge, leaving out Spirit both theoretically and experientially.

## Utilize Science

The scientific method, especially its experimental and inter-subjective components, can contribute a lot to spirituality by establishing it as a scientifically solid field. One observes others meditate, one experiences meditation by doing it, one shares, compares and confirms his or her results of meditation with other meditators—and the whole field of meditation is supported by scientific evidence and rigor.

You have a body, you have a mind, you are essentially Spirit. The world consists of many perspectives, including the scientific one. By transcending and including science in the process of our spiritual growth and unfolding, we are supporting and accelerating it.

From the practical standpoint, devices such as biofeedback, neurofeedback, brainwave entrainment and various tools for correlating brain waves and states of consciousness are all giving us hope for the emergence of a happy marriage between science and spirituality in the name of well-being, transformation and awakening.

Spirit X

#29

# Utilize Technology for Spiritual Growth and Unfolding

By utilizing here we mean practical application which is a blend of deep appreciation, and cognitive and spiritual discernment. From a spiritual standpoint, technology can be seen as a beautiful paradox inherent to human condition: thank God for technology and technology alone won't save us. Not only that technology alone won't save us but, given its accelerating speed and power, trusting and relying on technology alone can take us in a scary dystopian direction.

We truly live in the digital age. By that we mean that not only do we regularly use technology as a tool, but that technology informs and influences all other fields of human existence. The digital age influences the way we spend our time, energy and money, the way we connect and interact with each other, the way we raise our children, even the way we think, see the world and act toward ourselves, others and the world. In other words, the digital age, at this point of human evolution, determines who we are as a species. Instead of following blindly the digital progress or ne-

## Utilize Technology

gating it and resisting its benefits, we suggest that spiritual practitioners have a wise, co-creative relationship with the digital age: by using cognitive and spiritual discernment, we can use technology for the noble purposes.

Smart phones, personal computers, Alexa, Siri, smart homes, self-driving cars, artificial intelligence, virtual reality—it's all fine and dandy, but the truth is: our technological progress is way ahead of our moral and spiritual progress. Technologically, we are a very advanced and sophisticated civilization which cannot be said about us morally and spiritually. As long as we have powerful technology created and used by morally and spiritually undeveloped people, we are collectively facing a huge danger. Accelerated technological growth has to be accompanied with corresponding psycho-spiritual, cultural and social growth.

On a positive note, technology can support, enhance and accelerate spiritual growth and unfolding like no other field and activity. Recent breakthroughs in using smart phones, personal computers, the Internet, brain wave technology, augmented reality, virtual reality and artificial intelligence for well-being, transformation and awakening gives us hope that the happy marriage between technology and self-transformation can bring our individual and collective lives to yet unimaginable levels.

# Spirit X

The Holy Trinity of the digital revolution—smart phone, personal computer and the Internet—clearly show us the basic features of the digital age, and how it can be utilized for spiritual growth and unfolding.

Think of the smart phones—the vast majority of people in the developed global world have their smart phone with them all the time. Actually, they have them on them, almost all the time. Why don't we use that device mindfully, for our well-being, transformation and awakening?

Think of a personal computer—the vast majority of people in the developed world have that device at home (or with them). What do you do in front of it and with it? Any well-being, transformation or even awakening stuff?

Finally, the Internet connects us vastly and quickly and provides an extraordinary amount of information that can be used for well-being, transformation and awakening. Rather than complaining about the digital age—which spiritual practitioners often do—it is wise to acknowledge it and to use it mindfully for higher purposes.

The Internet is the product of global consciousness, envisioned to connect us on a mass scale and global level, and to serve as a platform for fast access and exchange of information. What can one say against global connectivity and sharing information? However, the culture of the Internet is not global, it is rather tribal, ethnocentric and sociocentric. Within the Internet as a global container, we have various individuals and groups at odds with each other. While technologically we were ready for the Internet, morally, psychologically, socially and politically we are still divided, and division often leads to conflict. However, by raising our moral and spiritual frequency, the general culture of the Internet can be transformed for the better.

Let's bring more kindness to the Internet. Now we understand the words of Dalai Lama that his religion is kindness.

Let's transform the digital world by bringing to it our higher individual and collective frequency. We know better than quarreling with each other on the Internet. Let's use the digital world to connect, share, support and Unite. And, indeed, to transform and awaken.

SPIRIT X

## #30
## TRANSFORM YOUR RELATIONSHIP WITH NEGATIVITY

And then there is all the negativity we hold towards the body, mind and the world. You are not happy with or even ashamed of your body. You are dealing with tough problems with your body and you don't see a way out. Your negative thoughts and moods are overwhelming and you cannot take it any more. The political and social scene is unstable, upsetting and corrupted and you feel disempowered about the world. Take a deep breath, my friend. One of the biggest promises of being on the spiritual path is a radical transformation of negativity. Or, we should say "negativity."

Whenever you label something as "positive" or "negative" you are giving too much power to your mind and falling into the dualistic trap: "I want this" and "I don't want this." And that is a sure way to continue the cycle of suffering inherent to ego-identification.

# Transform Your Relationship with Negativity

Whenever your notice negativity arising in your mind-body... slow down. Take few deep breaths. Into the belly, and out. Into the belly, and out. The key is to retrain your mind-body in relationship with negativity. Instead of pushing away everything which is negative regarding body-mind-world, gently acknowledge it, or even welcome it, like having a chat with an old friend. Have a coffee or tea with the Negative. Once you acknowledge it and welcome it—instead of pushing it into the unconscious—your relationship with negativity will radically transform. Negativity becomes "negativity."

Start by softening your relationship to yourself
and the world
Focus on your body sensations
Allow both comfort and discomfort
Don't get wrapped up in the dualistic mind
Focus on your mind
Simply watch it
Without labeling your thoughts
Allow the world as it is
At least for the purposes of this exercise
Beyond Positive and Negative
There is Peace
There is Your True Self.

# Spirit X

Good day—I welcome you.
Bad day—I welcome you, I don't complain about you, I work with you.

My imperfect body—I acknowledge you, I accept you, and possibly transform you from that place.

The pain in my knee—I feel you, I am not pushing you away, I am not labeling you as negative, by accepting you I transform you.

My monkey mind—let's have a coffee, let's slow down together.

Donald Trump—I acknowledge you; you are an expression of deeper unconscious currents, let's work through it together.

Hillary Clinton—I acknowledge you, you are an expression of deeper unconscious currents, let's work though it together.

The world crisis—I am not scared, I am inspired to working with you.

Relative Samsara—pleasures and pains, likes and dislikes, wins and loses, good days and bad days, us and them, life and death—I don't judge you, I welcome you.

Absolute Samsara—the endless cycle of birth, death and rebirth—I welcome you and by doing that I am beyond you.

## Transform Your Relationship with Negativity

I am Free.

When negative becomes "negative," you become You.

Welcome to your True Self.

# #31
# OVERCOME MATERIALISM

Although the approach in this book is to show how self (inner dimension) and the world (outer dimension) can be utilized as a way to deeper spiritual life and re-discovery of the True Self, the truth is that, ultimately, there is no boundary between self and the world, inner and outer, within and without. In this book, we approached the seeming self-world boundary (since it the how the world appears to the ego)—just in order to elegantly dissolve it. So, although in this part of the book we discuss various ways of how the world can be used for Self-Realization—it is, also, imperative not to fall into materialistic tendencies while doing it.

For many practitioners, it is exactly materialistic beliefs, habits and behaviors that prevent them from experiencing deeper Peace, Bliss and Self-Realization. In the present day spiritual world, there are three forms of materialism that have to be overcome: spiritual materialism, scientific materialism and economic materialism.

Spiritual materialism is a belief that your ultimate self

is your separate self, ego. The inherent problem with ego-identification is that it narrows life into narcissistic obsession with I-me-mine. In that case, spirituality becomes a way of ego-feeding and navigating and manipulating reality to maintain one's happiness. Although a certain degree of happiness can be found and experienced that way—any spirituality that feeds the ego is, on a long run, nothing but the continuation of suffering. That's why ego-transcendence is a real cornerstone of Spirit X. At the core of its (seeming and fleeting) structure, ego-identification is a sense of lack and lack just feeds the cycle of unfulfilled desire and suffering.

We live in a time when it is easy to get spiritual results fairly quickly. Teachings, techniques and resources are available to us like never before. That's why the view that ego-transcendence is reserved only for special ones and the ones with a good karma is simply not true and very disempowering. Ego-transcendence is everyone's potential and, like every other mastery, requires some effort. Mystifying ego-transcendence won't help anyone, especially in the times when it is becoming a necessity due to the complexities of the modern world, the acceleration of change and evolution, and the urgency to address global problems and issues. As we stated earlier: "You can do this and be That!"

Close your eyes, my friend

# Spirit X

Notice the Absence of the separate self
Be the Presence of your True Self.
Thanks.

☼

Ask loudly:"Who am I?"
Inquire quietly: "Who am I?"
Rest as the "answer."
It doesn't hurt if the questioner dissolves.
Thanks.

☼

The biggest gift you can give yourself, others, the world, and the Divine, is the gift of Presence.

☼

Scientific materialism, posited by natural sciences, is a belief that science is the ultimate teaching about Reality and that matter—the physical level of reality—is what is ultimately real. It is clear that in this worldview, there is no room for spirit and other important human activities such as arts, morals, love, justice, etc. When science becomes scientism, it locks people's minds in a view that is reductionistic and materialistic, and does not acknowledge the higher realms of Reality and Spirit. We have enough scientific and spiritual evidence to conclude and realize that Reality is a spectrum from matter to life to mind to soul to Spirit. From a spiritual standpoint, reducing reality to matter simply limits our basic human richness, flourishing and reaching our ultimate potential.

✺

We live in integral and holistic times, there is no reason to hold on one's discipline, doctrine or belief system when it comes to the Truth about Reality. There is science, but there are also arts and morals. There are politics and economics, but there are also environmentalism, quantum physics and spirituality. The Truth is rich, multidimensional and spectrum-like. All the disciplines touch and offer the Truth from different perspectives. The uniqueness and ultimate value of genuine spirituality is that it points to and opens avenues to the Ultimate Truth—the ultimate and unmanifest realm of our being and Reality.

✺

> Close your eyes, my friend
> Bring your full attention to the Heart
> And tell me
> What is ultimately real?

✺

Economic materialism is a belief that acquiring, collecting and consuming objects will make one ultimately happy. Economic materialism overemphasizes the importance of our economic and financial being. The trap of economic materialism and its consumerism is that it never delivers its promise, since no amount of objects can make one fully happy.

☼

How much stuff do you need to be happy?
How much money do you need to be happy?
The thing is, happiness is not that cheap.

☼

When we objectify everything, it is just a matter of time when we start objectifying human beings on a large scale. And that exactly is one of the biggest pathologies of the modern world.

☼

*(I Can't Get No) Satisfaction.* No wonder this The Rolling Stones song and vibration resonated with so many people.

☼

The underlying belief of all three forms of materialism is the belief in the spiritual ego, scientific ego or possessions-collecting ego—ego nevertheless.

☼

Within materialism—an endless cycle of trying and unfulfilled desire.

Beyond materialism—Absolute Subject within which all phenomena arise, shine and dissolve; your and universal True Self, and Peace and Happiness-Bliss inherent to it.

✧

Transcend your ego, my friend. It's that simple.

✧

"I can get, yes, Happiness-Bliss."

# #32
# OWN YOUR POWER

The situation regarding power in our post-modern world may be characterized as an unproductive paradox: those who have power, too often misuse it out of greed, arrogance and ignorance, and those who should step into the power, avoid doing it. This is not to say that everyone in a position of power or no power is behaving that way, but, in general, the world is stuck in this unproductive situation regarding power.

We have seen it so many times: power gets misused and suffering is caused to individuals, groups, nations and humankind. Politics, the economy, family and intimate relationships are full of examples where power is used in demeaning, oppressive and destructive ways. The reason, at least from a spiritual perspective, this is happening is a combination of hurt, trauma, unconscious, greed, arrogance, unpolished egos, outdated social and cultural habits and policies, and, most importantly, ignorance.

As a result, the vast majority of people in the present day world see power in a negative way. To make the whole situation with power even worse and more confusing—power is often demonized, portrayed that as soon as one assumes the position of power, one loses his or her mind and acts in an oppressive, corrupt and even self-destructive manner. Although this demonizing attitude towards power is completely understandable—given the damage this kind of power caused—the truth is that this is only the pathological effect of power. The tricky truth about power is—and this is where this topic is of crucial importance—we won't be able to move forward as a species unless we radically reconsider power and reintroduce healthy aspects of power into our lives, both individually and collectively, both internally and externally. Power has done a lot of damage, yet power is necessary for us to heal and move forward. Let's not throw the baby out with the bath water.

One of the main reasons why it is so difficult to heal our relationship with power and to reintroduce it into our lives and the world, is that in the present day post-modern egalitarian world, hierarchies are seen as a negative and oppressive phenomenon. "I am at the top, I am better than you, you are not worthy, I am going to use you like an object and oppress you." Welcome to the world of oppressive hierarchies that has caused a lot of suffering throughout human civilization. However, there are growth hierarchies, too: "I am at the top, and I am helping other fellow humans to be at the same level or at least to grow." Being at the top can also mean that you are helping others to get there and to grow and that you care about humanity as a whole. Brothers and sisters, it is time to acknowledge, reintroduce and utilize growth hierarchies.

# Spirit X

The spiritual significance of growth hierarchies is that they can be used like a stairway from our humanity to our Divinity, and indeed, embrace of our humanity from that absolute place. Once ego-transcendence becomes a widespread phenomenon, we will witness radical changes on this planet. Growth hierarchies can be one of the main vehicles for that to happen.

Like with many other maps and phenomena, the key is to approach power in a spectrum-like fashion. You have a body, you have a mind, you have a soul, you are essentially Spirit.

What is the power of the human body? To be healthy, strong and flexible. From a spiritual standpoint, it is imperative to keep the body powerful since it is our physical home in this dimension.

What is the power of the human mind? To be clear, to hold a right mindset and a right worldview, to hold a bigger picture and vision, to be synthetic and evolutionary, to discern and to be practical. A powerful mind is a prerequisite for a successful spiritual life since mind is the lens through which we see ourselves and the world and because messy mind can turn into a main obstacle on the spiritual path.

What is the power of trans-egoic soul? To withstand this dimension, to re-member Divine and spiritual evolution through wisdom and love, to be devoted to Liberation, and to accomplish its mission of finally being one with God.

And finally, what is the power of Spirit?
It is the power to Be.

Yes, my friend, the highest power is the power of Being—and it is identical to Peace. Radiant Peace, vibrant Peace, alive Peace. Peace that dances within itself and doesn't need anything outside of itself.

> Close your eyes
> Notice that before you are body
> And before you are mind
> You simply Are.
> Rest as Being
> Be
> You are Being-Power-Peace.

Although the vast majority of people on this planet, at this point of human evolution, are interested in other kinds of power than the power of Being, it is a hopeful indication that the best-selling book of our times is entitled "The Power of Now."

# Spirit X

✺

There is a also power in various dimensions of the human realm, such as family, institutional, social, political or virtual power. It is power that deals with our collective being. The imperative here is to access that power mindfully, skillfully and with integrity. The more trans-egos in the world, the better. This is, also, the area where the lens of growth hierarchies is of crucial importance.

✺

A word of empowerment: Not only that you are powerful, but you Are Power. Simply Be.

✺

May we reprogram our relationship with Power, both within and without, both individually and collectively, and use it to co-create a more soulful and spiritual civilization.

# # 33
# Don't Get Distracted

We come to this realm to taste Liberation and re-member who and what we truly are, but the vast majority of us get easily distracted. Tits, butts, sex, booze, drugs, status, fame, fortune, cars, houses, expensive travel, career, tech, global capitalism—the list is long of phenomena that can distract us on the path and catch our attention into negative attachments. But, likewise, sex, relationships, family, work, career, fortune, tech, purpose, spiritual path—the list is long of how being-in-the-world can be utilized for noble purposes and spiritual growth and unfolding.

Says Yes! to the world, without getting distracted and collapsing into bondage. You are That.

The world is both an immediate portal to Heaven and a stairway to Heaven. You can approach the world as a Gateless Gate into the Heaven of your True Self, or you can evolve into your, and our, Divinity. We suggest you do both. In terms of cultivating our spirit and accessing the formless, the world is the portal to one-without-a-second immediacy of Spirit. In terms of cultivating our mind, the world is the step-by-step re-membering of our Divinity. By honoring and utilizing both formless and evolutionary form, both Spirit and mind, Spirit X practitioners practice and embody spiritual frequency worthy of the interesting times we live in.

#34

# SPIRIT X 1.0 READING COMPLETION CONGRATULATIONS!

Congratulations, my friend, you have completed reading Spirit X 1.0, which is an experiential synthesis of global spirituality tailored for the contemporary reader and practitioner. You should congratulate yourself. Truly! In the age of short attention spans, instant gratification and accelerating change, you took time to read the first part of our teaching. We truly appreciate the attention—and time and energy—you gave us. For further questions, help and deepening of your realization of this level, please contact us at www.anandamali.com/spiritx.

≷

Take a pause. Holy Pause. Congratulate yourself. Embrace, accept and honor wherever you are on the spiritual journey. Embrace, accept and honor wherever others are on the spiritual journey. Amen.

≷

Join is in the Spirit X 2.0, Part 3 whenever you are ready.

# #35
# COMMERCIALS 1.0

Spirit X: Where Life and Spirit Meet.

In the Now,
In the Next,
Spirit X.

Take a Holy Pause: Expand Your Mind and Open your Heart with Spirit X

The Spirit X Jester dancing to *Stayin' Alive* by Bee Gees.

Spirit X: Since Infinity

We would like to thank to our sponsors, without which Spirit X wouldn't be possible: your Attention.

Spirit X

# SPIRIT X 2.0

*To the Ones devoted to the spiritual path, spiritual evolution, God(dess) and Enlightenment.*

*To the Ones inspired to bring a higher Unity of Spirit and Life into the global world.*

*To the Ones who aspire to help others on the path.*

*To the Ones I Love.*

Spirit X

# Part III
# The Book of Ways

# Spirit X

# #36
# WAYS AND CODES

As we have already pointed out, ultimate Spirit is a unity of the unmanifest and manifest. As practitioners, it is essential that we glimpse and stabilize our attention in the unmanifest and ultimate, and, also, it is imperative to master the world of form. Ultimately, Spirit is One, a spontaneous and radiant unity of unmanifest and manifest (emptiness and form, consciousness and energy); but, from the standpoint of spiritual practice and human dimension in general, we strongly recommend practices designed to utilize both the unmanifest and manifest dimensions of Spirit. Spiritual Realization is an extraordinary jewel that reveals to us the Absolute, yet, in the age of rich, complex and evolving form—it is simply not enough. On the one hand, Realization is no longer a guarantee that one will be fully fulfilled—or even comfortable—in all areas and dimensions of one's life. On the other hand, a life immersed only in the form, only in the manifest realm, marked by ego-identification, is, from a spiritual standpoint, a life of suffering. Addressing both dimensions of Spirit is nowadays a necessity and that's what we do in Spirit X.

Spirit X 1.0 is an experiential global synthesis of spirituality tailored for the global practitioner. It offers numerous gentle and elegant ways that one can design a spiritual practice, live a spiritual life, transcend the ego and re-discover True Self, and Peace, Bliss and pure Awareness inherent to it.

Spirit X 2.0 is a more advanced level of the Spirit X teaching as it utilizes Ways and Codes for mastering both unmanifest and manifest dimensions of Spirit, in a way that brings the unity of spiritual practice and life to another level. Ways are the ultimate Ways of Liberation, ways we re-discover and re-member our True Self. Codes are the relative modes we exist meaningfully and skillfully in the multidimensional manifest world. Ways help us being-at-home in the ultimate-unmanifest reality, Codes help us being-at-home in the manifest world.

#37

# Master Ways

Ways are central to the teaching of Spirit X. They are paths and modes that release us into our True Self, absolute Freedom, ultimate Spirit and Reality. Ways are ways to Liberation, Self-Realization. The wisdom traditions have already given us many Ways. For instance, in the *Bhagavad Gita*, one of the core texts and teachings of Hinduism, there are four yogas or paths or ways: jnana yoga (yoga of wisdom or pure discrimination), bhakti yoga (yoga of devotion), karma yoga (yoga of selfless service), and raja yoga (royal yoga of physical, psychological and spiritual exercise). The *Tao Te Ching*, the foundation written source of Taoism, offers us a manual for living in alignment with the Tao (the Way things are and unfold) with an emphasis on wei wu wei, often translated as "doing not-doing," but best understood as a spontaneous action or non-egoic expression of the Way. In Buddhism the central Ways are ones of meditation, compassion and tantra. In Christianity the central Ways are prayer and service. Spirit X as a spiritual teaching expands the number of Ways we can taste our True Self and Liberation as we live the life of Realization and Service.

At first, Ways appear to be a spiritual journeys towards higher reality or to a deeper place within ourselves. To-

# SPIRIT X

wards the end, we re-discover that Ways are actually journeyless journeys, rideless rides, we realize that the Way has always been below our feet. Realization and Liberation are Here and Now, if we just cultivate the Eye of Spirit, see it and be it. The spiritual journey follows a pattern: first, one seeks God, Higher Reality or Peace, with an emphasis on seeking; next, one re-discovers the ever-present True Self beyond seeking, beyond grasping and desiring, beyond the cycle of birth, death and rebirth; and finally, after Realization, one enters a life of Service and Expression. The Ways of Spirit X follow this same pattern, release us into the Freedom that we already are and help us polish our unique gifts of Service and Expression.

In short, the three-fold structure of the Ways is as following: 1) practice-seeking, 2) Realization and 3) Service-Expression. For the vast majority of spiritual seekers, seeking is a necessary step before Realization. Desiring, striving, seeking is simply inherent to the human condition and ego-identification. Some forms of spiritual seeking, such as ascending, can be relatively blissful and productive to an extent; however, spiritual seeking is just a form of subtle suffering. As long as you are seeking, even for spiritual enlightenment, and as long as your center of gravity is in being a seeker—you are identifying with the sense of lack and are prolonging suffering. Realization is a Liberation from body-mind-world and a re-discovery of your ever-present True Self. It is the end of seeking as a major mode of being and the beginning of a life of Service and Expression. Service here refers to the service to transformation of consciousness, spiritual evolution, God and Spirit. Expression here refers to the quality of That such as Being, Consciousness, Bliss, Peace, Stillness, Wisdom, Compassion, Love, Evolution, Transparency, Clarity, Spontaneity, Flow, Receptivity, Creativity, Enlightened Humor, Fierce Grace, etc.

Within the Ways there are two possible kinds of Realization: initial and abiding. In other words, you can glimpse your True Self or you can abide as your True Self. In Spirit X, we hold—in order to make Realization possible and digestible for as many people as possible—that all you need in terms of Realization is a glimpse (with the hope that the further process of Realization permeating body-mind-world will continue and be completed). If abiding Realization happens—even better. Spirit X as a teaching provides methods for both glimpsing and stabilizing Realization.

Realization is not complete unless we fully embrace our humanity, both in terms of universal structure (we are all born, eat, sleep, cry, laugh, get older and die), and our unique individuality (I am good at this, and not that good at that, this is uniquely me). Realization of our empty, pure nature is just a transcendence-part of Realization. The embrace-part—and the completion of Realization—consists of fully embracing both the universal and individual components of our human nature.

# Spirit X

Realization and Service are two sides of the same coin. There is no genuine Realization without a noble desire—out of abundance and not out of lack—to help others experience the same and to serve the evolution of consciousness. Also, Realization comes with a sense of Radiance, so whether you want it or not—you radiate That, you emanate That, you express That. Because You are That.

It is with Service and Expression that our unique individual traits re-emerge in the human realm, this time not as ego features but as unique vehicles of Spirit itself. For instance, if, before Realization, you had a good sense of humor, you can use humor Now (after Awakening) for the purpose of awakening others. Or, if you, before Realization, had a strong and healthy body, you can use the body Now to sustain and express your Realization and inspire others to approach Realization in the integral body-mind-spirit fashion.

Master the Ways. Sounds complicated and reserved only for the chosen ones, doesn't it? But, aren't we able to master various skills during our lifetime? We master cooking, sports, playing the piano, raising children, studying philosophy, leading countries, meditating, landing on the Moon, etc. Why not bring our individual and collective spiritual mastery to the next level? The truth is, my friend, we have no other way than to go deeper spiritually, or, as we put it in Spirit X, to master Ways. On the one hand, why not, since spiritual Awakening is now available for the first time in human history on a large scale; teachings and practices across traditions are available globally to us; psychology, sciences and technology are helping the process, and more and more people are genuinely interested in spirituality and Awakening. On the other hand, we are facing some scary stuff as a species, such as global pandemic, environmental crisis, nuclear crisis, economic inequality and collapse, political tension, greed, hatred and ignorance on a large scale; we are not even quite sure at this point who we are, individually and collectively. Those negative revolutions are making it necessary for us to Wake Up. So master Ways, my friend. Why not? And if not now, then when? Honestly, what better to do in the human form and human dimension?

There is no reason to mystify Liberation, Enlightenment, Awakening, Self-Realization, or whatever you want to call it. It is simply your natural state, who and what you truly are. All that needs to be done is to elegantly remove over-identification with body-mind-world. And to enjoy the Bliss and Inspiration of a Life of Service and Expression.

This doesn't mean that, after Realization, our humanity is somehow erased and left behind, like a space ship leaving the Earth. One still eats, sleeps, has emotions, gets sick, experiences "good days" or "bad days", one still "dies". Our humanity is transcended and included into Realization and Service. Realization does not erase humanity and "negativity", it just provides a more effective perspective to deal with it, embrace it, or improve it, or be at peace with our humanity and "negativity" inherent to it.

The beautiful thing about Realization is that it permeates not only the body and mind but the whole world and all possible worlds. The world—and all worlds—is your body. Or, the world—and all possible worlds—are your thoughts.

A practical note on how to utilize the Ways. In our present-day global spiritual community various practitioners have various typologies and temperaments. Unique individual preferences are included into spiritual teachings. Some practitioners prefer meditation, some dive deeper via prayer, and some open themselves through meaningful and selfless work. In that sense, choose a Way or Ways that work for you and open you towards your True Self.

Also, we live in integral and holistic times, which means that the more integral you get with your practice and service, the better results and enlightened life you will have. So alongside the Ways, we strongly suggest doing some practices discussed in Part 1—meditation, prayer, contemplation, satsang, etc.—as well as touching the basics of your being and reality such as body-mind-spirit cross-training, connecting with others in person and virtually, communing with nature, meaningful cultural and social engagements, etc. Create your own spiritual practice and life, my friend. Teachings, practices and tools are available.

## #38
# THE WAY OF MEDITATION

The Way of Meditation utilizes one of the best practices from the wisdom traditions and makes it our center of gravity and Home. Meditation has been a royal path to Liberation and our True Self for centuries. In the modern world, meditation is widespread and is becoming a mainstream phenomenon. Spirit X as a teaching utilizes the importance, power and presence of meditation.

Meditation has many benefits for our health and well-being: it relaxes the nervous system, strengthens the immune system, improves blood circulation, reduces stress and chronic pain, helps with the symptoms of depression, anxiety, addiction and cancer, brings clarity to our lives, and much more. The benefits of meditation as a practice for our separate self are literally endless. However, the real purpose of meditation is that it reveals to us the depth of our being and Reality and our True Self. Although in Spirit X we acknowledge the importance of meditation for health and well-being, we strongly suggest the use of meditation for deeper spiritual purposes.

# The Way of Meditation

At the beginning of the Way of Meditation the key is to assume the meditation posture regularly. Meditation posture stills the body and mind, balances our subtle energy system and reveals to us our nature as open, spacious awareness. The result is the Bliss of being inherent to the meditation posture which is harder to realize with other spiritual practices. This Bliss comes from the science and art of the posture itself. Feeling good without any external causes, simply feeling good for the heck of it—ah, the pure Bliss and simplicity of the meditation posture.

There are two basic types of meditation: meditation with form and formless meditation. Meditation with form stills our mind by focusing on various types of form such as the breath, an object, an image, a mantra, or an archetype. Formless meditation is an advanced type of meditation that reveals to us the empty nature of our being and Reality; we simply rest as Spirit and witness the coming and going of various physical, mental and subtle forms of manifest reality.

In accordance with this, there are two qualities that we emphasize in the Way of Meditation: alertness and relaxation. When we meditate we can either concentrate on (or be alert to) something—the breath, an object, an image, a word, a deity, an archetype—or we can relax into what is and rest as pure Spirit. So when you meditate, explore those two qualities: alertness and relaxation. Notice how alert you are, notice how relaxed you are. What a beautiful paradox and richness of our spiritual being: alert, alive, relaxed and vast all at the same time.

The real benefits of the Way of Mediation happen when we bring those qualities of alertness and relaxation into our life. Let us not forget that in Spirit X the real purpose of all formal practices is to dissolve the seeming boundary between spiritual practice and life. So, meditate and be alert and relaxed; live your life and be alert and relaxed. Once alertness and relaxation are brought into life and everyday activities, one becomes either a vessel of Spirit or rests as an expression of Being itself. The ego is transparent and the life of Spirit starts. The true secret of meditation is that the real meditator is not you as separate self but You as Absolute Self or Reality or pure Spirit. Reality meditates itself and you are invited to join. The Way of Meditation reveals this larger than life secret of meditation.

The real goal of meditation is to gently and elegantly dissolve the meditator.

In terms of the three-part structure of the Ways, the Way of Meditation is a perfect expression of it. The meditation-practitioner cultivates a regular meditation practice.

## The Way of Meditation

Make sure you create a space at home dedicated to mediation practice only. Meditate on your own and with others. Get help from qualified teachers and mentors about various meditation techniques and tricks. At its core, meditation is a pleasurable practice and—although, at times, we may experience physical pain or face our demons on the cushion—once the regularity of meditation practice is established, it will become a highlight of your day and will be easy to keep going.

And, one day it happens: you finish your meditation, you leave the cushion, you go on with your day, and the meditation continues. Amen.

Meditation is one of the superb Ways that lead to Realization. For the vast majority of practitioners throughout centuries, Realization is a spontaneous event. That means that it may, or may not, happen on the meditation cushion. As they say in Zen: "Enlightenment is an accident; practice makes you accident prone." The more you meditate, the more you are increasing the possibility of Realization.

Meditation is a powerful practice and it is easy to get attached to it. And attachments—even to royal spiritual practices—don't help Realization. In that regard, it is advisable that, at the mature stages of the Way of Meditation, one meditates without being attached to meditation. If you meditated—okay. If you haven't meditated—okay. If meditation was successful—okay. If meditation was challenging —okay. This attitude will certainly increase the possibility of Realization.

In the Way of Meditation, after Realization meditation becomes spontaneous. It is not a practice any more but a Way of Life. In the case of abiding Realization, one simply lives the Way of Meditation. In the case of initial Realization, one stabilizes the Realization by continuing with the meditation practice (in a non-attached way), and by cultivating the qualities of being alert and relaxed in everyday life. Formless meditation and inquiry can be of help here for stabilizing Realization.

The climax of the Way of Meditation is certainly Service and Expression. At this stage, one is alert-relaxed, inspired and qualified to help others master the Way of Meditation. One is the embodiment of meditation, and an inspiration for others to pursue and achieve the same. Whether you guide and inspire others on how to meditate, or simply radiate with your presence the qualities of meditation— with Service and Expression of the Way of Meditation you yourself become an endless Nectar of Wisdom and Love, and are offering a noble service to others and the world.

# The Way of Meditation

Practices and modules that support the Way of Meditation are meditation, contemplation, inquiry, body-mind-spirit cross training, communing with nature, science, technology and silence.

The Way of Meditation starts on the cushion with eyes closed and ends with eyes open, hands open and Heart wide open full of Love, embracing all possible worlds.

Meditate... open your eyes... Be.
The real Meditator is Reality.

SPIRIT X

## #39
# THE WAY OF AWARENESS

The Way of Awareness is both a gradual and a direct way of realizing Awareness as the core of one's being and Reality. The main advantage of this Way is that it can be done as a formal practice (meditation, contemplation) or as an informal, spontaneous, on-the-spot practice, suitable for modern-day spiritual practitioners. In a gradual version of this Way, one is first aware of body, then mind, then aware of Awareness and, finally, is Awareness as such. In a direct version of this Way one goes directly to the awareness of Awareness.

The Way of Awareness utilizes an amazing and often overlooked fact about the human condition: right Here, right Now, you are simply aware. You may be aware of pain, or pleasure, or thoughts, or various situations you find yourself in—but the fact is that you are aware. Awareness is the container in which all of our experiences—whether positive of negative—appear. The exploration of this simple awareness is one of the most liberating practices available to us today.

The Way of Awareness moves one's center of gravity from being aware of something to being Awareness itself, by dis-

# The Way of Awareness

tinguishing—gradually or directly—between the content of awareness and Awareness itself.

Can you distinguish, right Here, right Now, between thought and Awareness?

You can try the following instructions in a formal setting, like a regular practice, or play with them during everyday life activities (opportunity to dissolve the boundary between life and practice from the very beginning).

Start with being aware of the body, not as an entity, but as a series of body sensations. Some of the body sensations are comfortable, and some are not. By embracing both comfort and discomfort—at least for the purposes of this Way—one goes beyond the dualistic mind and rests deeper. Awareness of the body provides freedom from the body and the embrace of it.

Continue with being aware of the mind, not as an entity, but as a series of thoughts, images, judgments, interpretations, stories and visions. Simply watch your mind. Awareness of the mind provides freedom from the mind and the embrace of it.

The next step is crucial on the spiritual path: be aware of Awareness. Pay attention to Attention. Look at the Looker. Observe the Observer. Who is ultimately aware of the whole world of manifestation? Be That.

One of the biggest tricks when it comes to the human condition is that we overlook and don't spiritually utilize the powerful and liberating fact that we are aware. After awareness of Awareness is practiced and established one makes one more step towards being nondual, spontaneous, self-manifesting Awareness, in which the last duality is finally dissolved.

The Way of Awareness can be practiced as a formal practice or gently introduced into daily living... until you are self-manifesting Awareness freely dancing within itself.

The first part of the process, being aware of and free from the body, dismantles one's attachment to the body, which plays a role in believing in the false sense of self, separated from others, the world and Spirit itself. Freedom from the body is just the beginning of the journey of liberating one's awareness from the spectrum of attachments.

The second part of this practice, being aware of and free from the mind, is an opportunity for ego-transcendence. Among the stream of thoughts, one particular thought gets our special attention—the thought of "I." Then we attach our story, preferences, likes and dislikes, to that thought

# The Way of Awareness

of "I," and the false sense of self is born and maintained through re-enforcing attachments again and again. Thus, the practice of being aware of the mind is an opportunity to be free from one's ego, too.

The crucial step in the process, being aware of Awareness, is an act of transcending the body-mind-world, and, in that respect, takes us beyond basic categories of mind, space and time. Beyond ego, beyond space and time—still You. Such is the spiritual journey. And that's still not the end.

The final step in the process dissolves the last duality between unmanifest Witness and manifest body-mind-world. All that is left is Awareness being aware of itself, Awareness dancing within itself, Awareness shining appropriately and skillfully through the body-mind-world.

For the direct approach of the Way of Awareness, one can go directly to being aware of Awareness. That act alone dissolves one into the pure Spirit.

And, yes, the Direct Path is profoundly right and simple: the wave is already 100% the ocean, there is no moment that the separate self is not already the Self, the cloud and the sky are one and the same, emptiness and form are not-two. And, it doesn't take any time to realize That: One without a second.

Who is aware of this moment? Be That.

Or, as my teacher, Mokshananda, used to point out to me gently: "To whom is this arising?" Or, "I don't need to do anything to be myself," or "Where do you go when you go to sleep?"

Aware of Awareness.

Radiant Awareness.

In terms of the three-part structure of the Ways—practice-seeking, Realization, Service-Expression—the Way of Awareness unfolds in the following fashion.

The Way of Awareness practitioner utilizes the Way of Awareness both formally and informally, both gradual-

## The Way of Awareness

ly and directly (depending on the practitioner's spiritual type). One of the major advantages of the Way of Awareness is that it can be practiced in the midst of the daily activities (aware of the body, aware of the mind, aware of Awareness) and that is certainly something to be utilized.

Across the traditions, the Way of Awareness—in its numerous forms—has a proven record of successfully leading practitioners to Realization. Within this Way, Realization can happen gradually or via a single, usually spontaneous, event, often as a result of a teacher's pointer. In the case of abiding Realization, one simply lives and breathes this Way and helps others in accordance with this Way. In the case of initial Realization, one continues with the practice and emphasizes the embodiment part (since embodiment is one of the best ways to stabilize Awakening).

In terms of Service and Expression, the Way of Awareness has a strong radiance component and skillful means component. The Way of Awareness produces a very clear, potent and radiant-silent Realization, as well as the effective and short skillful means, mostly pointers, for awakening others.

The Way of Awareness is one of the most suitable Ways for our global, busy and complex world, since it offers means that can be utilized at any time and any place. Very few ways across wisdom traditions can be this simple and effective.

# Spirit X

Practices and modules that support the Way of Awareness are inquiry, satsang, meditation, body-mind-spirit cross-training, work, science and silence.

Who am I? Live That.

# #40
# THE WAY OF THE SPIRITUAL WARRIOR

One can argue that in times of crisis, uncertainty and wild change, the last thing we need is warriorship. Yet, spiritual warriorship is warriorship of a specific kind and, actually, very appropriate, if not even necessary, in times like ours. Qualities such as courage, fearlessness, discipline, patience, commitment to the goal, serving something bigger than yourself, ultimate sacrifice, facing death, love, and awareness, are of incredible help for both Realization and Service-Expression. The Way of the Spiritual Warrior shows up in various forms across spiritual traditions, most notably in Tibetan Buddhism. In Spirit X teaching we honor various spiritual traditions and give the Way of Spiritual Warrior a modern touch and twist in the name of its full global appreciation, application and utilization.

The spiritual warrior "fights" the ultimate enemy: ignorance, both within and without. Ignorance is not knowing who and what you truly are and not realizing the essence of others and the world. Fueled by desire and fear, ignorance continues human suffering and samsara, the cycle of birth, death and rebirth.

# Spirit X

The Way of the Spiritual Warrior perfectly applies to the three-part structure of the Ways in Spirit X. Warriorship is applicable, if not necessary, for seeking-practice, Realization and Service-Expression.

The foundation stone of every Way is practice and effort. Very few people have realized their True Self without practice and making effort. Warrior-practitioner shows up in practice and brings courage to the removal of inner ignorance. Spiritual practice is not always an easy process, at times we need to leave our comfort zone—both internally and externally—and that is exactly when spiritual warriorship is handy in spiritual practice. At times we need to fight our inner demons, at times we need to work through our inner blockages. Bringing courage, discipline and patience to those situations is often the best thing we can do.

In the present day global world, the warrior-practitioner may experience lots of challenges coming from without. The materialistic world, lack of time and resources for practice, feeling alone on the path, the inertia of mind-body —all of these obstacles can be handled by embodying the warrior-practitioner attitude and energy.

The death the spiritual warrior is facing is ego-death. The ultimate internal task of the spiritual warrior is to let go of ego-identification.

# The Way of the Spiritual Warrior

When it comes to Realization, the Way of the Spiritual Warrior reveals to us the paradox of battling and seeking. At some point the Spiritual Warrior gives up the fight. Yes… gives up the fight. All the fighting, all the seeking, all the practice-improving, all the courage in the face of the negative, all the discipline—it's all in vain. The essence is not in fearless practice and effort, the essence is in surrendering to Here and Now and re-discovering the Stillness inherent to it. The Warrior paradoxically wins by surrendering into True Liberation. At the end of the fight, in the moment of ego-death, the Spiritual Warrior is victoriously on his knees with his palms together. "I get it, I get it. Thank you God. Liberation is in Here and Now, Stillness is in Here and Now, the removal of Ignorance happens in Here and Now, it's Here and Now," echoes through his body, mind and the whole universe.

Practice is great, Realization is even greater, but the ultimate point of warriorship is Service. The real juice of the Way of the Spiritual Warrior is in service to humanity, Divinity and the evolution of consciousness. We are really here to help and serve others, it's just that higher "Others" include us and the world. We are here to serve Spirit—and that's where the Way of Spiritual Warrior is timeless. In the age when Spirit is needed yet unrecognized, what else to be than be the spiritual warrior. When it comes to Service and Expression, everyone should be a spiritual warrior for at least a bit.

# Spirit X

⟫➤ ☮

Or, to play with David Bowie's song:
"We should be Warriors, just for one day."

⟫➤ ☮

When it's time to meditate and your mind is telling you to watch TV—remind yourself that you are on the Way of the Spiritual Warrior.

When it's time to practice and you feel like masturbating instead—remind yourself that you are on the Way of the Spiritual Warrior.

When you are scared of ego-death—remind yourself that you are on the Way of the Spiritual Warrior.

When it's time to break the attachment to practice-effort and to truly surrender—remind yourself that you are on the Way of the Spiritual Warrior.

When everyone around you is telling you that spirituality is bunch of BS—remind yourself that you are on the Way of the Spiritual Warrior.

When ignorance is getting wild in the world—remind yourself that you are on the Way of the Spiritual Warrior.

When Service to Spirit is an Inspiration and Empowerment—that's why you are on the Way of the Spiritual Warrior.

## The Way of the Spiritual Warrior

The energy of the Spiritual Warrior is White Fire, White Light.

The human realm is still marked by ignorance. What did you do today to remove ignorance, within and without?

Practices and modules that support the Way of the Spiritual Warrior are meditation, prayer, body-mind-spirit cross-training, work, purpose and technology.

Spiritual Warriors of the world, unite!

Bring spiritual evolution to the next level!

Practice, be courageous, surrender, be spiritually inspired and creative!

# #41
# THE WAY OF THE SPIRITUAL TRICKSTER

Jokes everywhere and on everything, nothing is holy, no difference between fake and real news, irony, sarcasm, funny and not that funny memes, everybody is right, nobody tells me what to do, all-pervading confusion—welcome to the challenging aspects of the present day world. And let me introduce you to the Trickster. And—to an extent—let me introduce you to Life.

⌘

The Trickster is a figure present in many myths, cultures and religions. In times of crisis, the Trickster shows up to show us the way via playful, rebellious and unconventional skillful means. The present day cultural scene is full of humor, laughter, comedy, jesters, funny social media memes and entertainment. Our youth gets the news and information filtered through humor and entertainment. For some of them it is the main contact with the real world. Although this process has many downsides, it can certainly be utilized for spiritual and awakening purposes. The Way of the Spiritual Trickster does exactly that.

⌘

# The Way of the Spiritual Trickster

One of the common features of the Trickster across myths, cultures and religions is that it challenges playfully and rebelliously the conventional world and behavior. What is the present day conventional reality from a spiritual standpoint? It is a set of beliefs and interpretations of reality that keep the conventional world intact. The core of those beliefs is the belief that one's real self is a separate self, ego. Other beliefs that accompany this core one are the belief that one can find ultimate happiness through collecting money and acquiring objects and stuff, the belief that reality is ultimately matter, the belief that death is an absolute end, etc.

The Spiritual Trickster knows very well that behind the veil of conventional reality lies the Sacred and he is not shy about tricking us out of the egoic spell. This wise-fool has tasted the deeper dimension of Reality and chooses funny, challenging, yet effective and appropriate for our times skillful means to help us do the same. Beyond the conventional world lies the Sacred, beyond egoic spell there is your infinite and eternal True Self—that's the wisdom and promise of the Spiritual Trickster. And if we can have some profound fun throughout the process, even better.

⌘

The Spiritual Trickster knows and utilizes the overlap between transgression and transcendence. Both processes point to the Great Beyond; transgression via sometimes wild and problematic breaking of moral and social norms, and transcendence via a more subtle and elegant means. The Spiritual Trickster uses more means of transcendence, but is aware that transgression may work in certain situations and for some people. The thing is that in the conventional world, the seeming boundaries may be difficult to break and release, and as the master of breaking and removing boundaries, the Spiritual Trickster shows up to do the noble and, at times, risky job.

⌘

The crazy wisdom of the Trickster: via challenge and transgression, beyond right and wrong, beyond duality, there is Bliss, Peace, and Oneness, there is You-Awareness.

⌘

The Trickster may come to you in many forms since essentially the Trickster is a shape-shifter. Externally, he or she can come to you as a friend that takes you Beyond via playfulness and laughter, as a crazy wisdom teacher, as a group that challenges conventional norms, as a rebel you secretly admire. Internally, he can come to you as a sense of humor, like a light and playful attitude towards Life, like a post-conventional lifestyle, like an inner-rebel and inner voice and wisdom. The way to Liberation is tricky and knowing how to recognize and listen to the Trickster—both externally and internally—may be quite an asset on the spiritual journey.

⌘

# The Way of the Spiritual Trickster

The Trickster shows up in the world when we reach the limits of a certain worldview and ways of living and being. Ego-identification, materialism and fear of death have served their noble purpose in human evolution and now it is time to create a new humankind and a new Earth. If you want to do it in a playful and post-conventional way—the Way of Spiritual Trickster is for you.

⌘

In terms of the three-part structure of the Ways, the Way of the Spiritual Trickster unfolds in the following fashion. When it comes to seeking-practice, the Way of Spiritual Trickster may not be the easiest path, but the nature of this Way is that it is a bit tricky. The Trickster-practitioner simply stays open to the Trickster within or without, since one of the main features of the Trickster is shape-shifting. Clearly, the Trickster-practitioner has a karmic preference for playfulness, breaking and releasing of rules and boundaries, post-conventional values and methods, rebellion, etc. The key at this stage is to recognize that the Trickster is taking you beyond conventional, ego-based reality and that he mediates between the human and the Divine.

⌘

When it comes to Realization, there is certainly a Trickster part to it. Realization has a funny side and funny Wisdom to it. It's Here and Now. Really? I mean, really? We seek just in order to realize that non-seeking is the point? And, it takes lifetimes to realize That. The Trickster-Realization

# Spirit X

is a funny and relieving Release beyond the karma of body-mind-world into your True Self. Its final response is Laughter. And its new beginning is Laughter.

⌘

Like with the Way of the Spiritual Warrior, the real juice of the Way of the Spiritual Trickster is in Service-Expression. The Awakened Trickster certainly does not lack skillful means. Actually, abundance and appropriateness of his skillful means (tricks) are his major strengths. One thing about the Trickster makes him appropriate, if not necessary, for our times: he knows how to get people's attention. The Trickster is literally the attention grabber and the attention shifter. And, in times like ours, when it's all about attention, he is the real Master. Once the Trickster has people's attention, he will playfully and skillfully point to the deeper dimension of their being and the True Self.

⌘

Meet the Trickster:

What's up Ladies and Gents
How is everyone today?
How are your conventional butts today?

So why don'ts we start from there
From your lazy, materialistic, conventional butts.

I invite you to bring your attention

## The Way of the Spiritual Trickster

to the place where your butt meets the chair
Your butt meeting the chair
Hmm, how nice
Your body meeting the thing
Yum
Life-object meeting the matter-object.
Rest there for a while.
Butt meeting the chair.

Now, we are going to shift our attention
To your mind
I want you to focus on your mind
And to produce the thought of a pink elephant
and the thought of a happy you
and the thought of a better world.

Now, we are going to bring our attention
to the Heart
and feel the Love
and Be the Love.

You are not going to tell me that
your butt on the chair
is more real than any thought or feeling of Love.

Why are you so caught up
in the materialistic world?
The real cheesecake is beyond it.

Go to your miserable lives
Do your boring jobs

# Spirit X

Go listen to fucking politicians
Go trust your president
And good luck.

I am going to have a drink
and then off to my
rendezvous with God.

And don't call on me
Unless you are
Ready to radically
Move your lazy conventional butts.

⌘

When was the last time someone or something tricked you into the deeper dimension of Life?

When was the last time you tricked someone into the deeper dimension of Life?

⌘

Meet the Trickster one more time:

What's up
Ladies and Gents
Here is THE proposal for you:
If you meet the folks
Who don't do psycho-spiritual work
Simply don't fuck them.

## The Way of the Spiritual Trickster

⌘

Remember Bugs Bunny, pop-culture most popular Trickster? "Eh… What's up, doc?"

⌘

The Spiritual Trickster says: "Spirit X, fuck yeah!"

⌘

Practices and modules that support the Way of the Spiritual Trickster are meditation, music, pop-culture, dance, movement, art and technology.

⌘

What's up Ladies and Gents?

SPIRIT X

## #42
# THE WAY OF BEAUTY

The Way of Beauty utilizes the aesthetical component of the human dimension and this universe. Not all universes are characterized by a strong aesthetical component. More than two thousand years ago, ancient Greek philosopher Plato realized the importance of Beauty in this realm. In his major teaching, the theory of ideas, the manifest realm is the emanation from three supreme ideas, Beauty, Truth and Goodness. The process of learning and, for that matter, the whole human life, is way of re-membering the realm of ideas.

Are you drawn to Beauty? Are you inspired by it? Do you aspire to bring it more into your life and the world? Then, the Way of Beauty is for you.

"Beauty is is in the eye of the beholder," we often hear when we talk about beauty, arts and taste. Although this statement points to the relative and subjective nature of beauty (what is beautiful for me may not be beautiful for you), from a spiritual standpoint this statement has a completely different meaning. If the beholder deepens his or her perspective and cultivates the Eye of Spirit—everything is beautiful, everything is an expression of the Beauty of Spirit. The closer we get to our True Self, the more beauty, internally and externally, is available to us. The climax of this process is seeing Beauty in everything, moment-to-moment. This aesthetical-spiritual process simply shows the importance and power of shifting perception (rather than endlessly trying to manipulate what is perceived and the field of perception). True Beauty lies in the perception, not in the perceived. So, my friend, take responsibility for deepening your perception and Spirit will reward you with a lot of Beauty. Beauty is in the Eye of Spirit.

If you feel that the Way of Beauty fits you, start with simply realizing that there is Beauty in the human condition and this universe, and be grateful for it. Cultivate your relationship with Beauty. Make it a contemplative and creative relationship. Observe Beauty and appreciate Beauty. Create Beauty. Acknowledge that there is outer and inner beauty.

To cultivate your relationship with outer beauty—visit beautiful places (both in terms of nature and human civilization), surround yourself with beauty, appreciate or even create art, discover what art opens you to a deeper dimension and qualities such as Awe, Peace and Inspiration.

To cultivate your relationship with inner beauty—acknowledge the inherent beauty of the inner universe. Listen to your favorite song or music and notice what is hap-

# Spirit X

pening internally in terms of feelings and moods, read your favorite book or type of literature and notice what kind of state of consciousness it produces. Close your eyes, meditate and acknowledge the subtle beauty of images, visions, noble feelings and sounds. Be open to Beauty as a profound spiritual experience.

Gently close your eyes. Fully rest. Rest as the Source. Rest as You. Isn't it beautiful? Or even beyond it?

The beauty of the human body: observe it, contemplate it, love it, cultivate it, be it.

The beauty of your favorite song: honor it, celebrate it, share it with others.

The beauty of the arts: appreciate it, create it, share it with others.

The beauty of the intellect: marvel at it, cultivate it, share it with others.

The beauty of spiritual insight: so relieving and liberating.

The beauty of spiritual vision: ah, beyond this world. Cannot help but act out of it.

The Beauty beyond Beauty of your True Self: no words to describe it. Share it with others.

At final instance, surrender to Beauty: allow your mind-body to be blown away by inner and outer beauty; train your mind-body to be deeply affected by and responsive to Beauty. At this stage your relationship to Beauty is therapeutic (beauty is an important part of your well-being and health) and spiritual (beauty is leading you towards your True Self). At this stage, you are also inspired and deeply moved by Beauty. In the final stage of the Way of Beauty, one simply realizes the Beauty beyond Beauty. The contemplation and creation of Beauty dissolves subject-object duality. At the end of the Way of Beauty there is only Beauty happening, no subject to contemplate it and no object to be contemplated, no subject to create and object to be created. Just Spirit being itself in its own eternal Beauty.

In terms of the three part structure of the Ways, the Way of Beauty unfolds in the following fashion. The Beauty spiritual practitioner centers his or her practice around Beauty, that is, appreciation, contemplation and creation of Beauty. At this stage, Beauty is the practitioner's Ideal. Also, at this stage we recommend doing spiritual practices such as meditation and contemplation, with a Beauty twist to it. What is beautiful about meditative and contemplative states? What is beautiful about spiritual aspiration? What is

# SPIRIT X

beautiful about spiritual practice?

As for the Realization part of the three-part structure of the Ways, the key is to completely surrender to Beauty and to allow Beauty to take you to its source: Beauty beyond Beauty that embraces Everything. Realization within the Way of Beauty can be enhanced and supported by formless practices such as formless meditation, inquiry or satsang.

The Service-Expression part of the Way of Beauty is the real juice of this Way. After stabilizing Realization, one lives, breathes and expresses Beauty. One embodies Beauty by fully allowing it to be expressed and shared via various skillful means such as breathing, gazing, simply being, appreciating, gardening, making music, writing, teaching, helping others, serving the world and much more.

Practices and modules that support the Way of Beauty are appreciation of life, arts and the full spectrum of Beauty; creativity, meditation, contemplation, communing with nature, culture, pop-culture, music and technology.

Beauty beyond Beauty: no words to describe it.

# #43
# THE WAY OF MAHAVATAR BABAJI

The Way of Mahavatar Babaji is the Way of Liberation and Expression with and through an archetypal deity. Archetypes are the subtle seeds out of which the manifest world emanates, they are both empty and full, simultaneously beyond and within manifestation. Alongside deities, archetypes include Platonic forms of Truth, Beauty and Goodness, the perfect primordial number, the perfect primordial sound, the perfect primordial vibration and more. On a relative level, archetypes abide in the high subtle realm of reality and influence from there the evolution of consciousness; on an ultimate level, archetypes, like everything else, arise in your own Awareness. In the Spirit X teaching, we approach archetypes in the 2nd person (often as the Great Thou), bring them into 1st person (I) and go beyond 2nd and 1st person unity (Ultimate I).

❊

Mahavatar Babaji is a legendary figure in world spirituality. This leader of the leaders, the teacher of the teachers, has been assisting prophets, teachers, gurus and leaders since times immemorial in the evolution of consciousness and East-West integration. Often hidden and mysterious, rarely

# Spirit X

transparent and visible in the human dimension, Mahavatar Babaji was globally revealed by Paramahansa Yogananda in his bestselling classic *The Autobiography of a Yogi*. In recent spiritual history, he first appeared to Yogananda's teacher's teacher Lahiri Mahasaya, initiating him in the ancient teaching of Kriya Yoga and giving him the task of sharing it with modern world. The crucial part of this teaching and broader vision was to bring together yogic spiritual practice and householder duties and responsibilities. Mahavatar Babaji then appeared to Yogananda's teacher, Sri Yukteswar, instructing him to write a book that would point to the underlying unity between Christian and Hindu scriptures—which became *The Holy Science* —and establish the middle path of activity and spirituality, and indeed, announcing to him that he will send him a disciple who would bring East-West integration to the next level. Finally, he appeared to Yogananda himself announcing to him that he is the chosen one to spread the message of Kriya Yoga to the West. Far from being reduced to only this lineage and Kriya Yoga, Mahavatar Babaji is one of the most important archetypes when it comes to long-term human spiritual evolution and the never-ending East-West integration.

How cool and prophetic is it that Mahavatar Babaji is on the cover of one of the most important records of all time, The Beatles' *Sgt. Pepper's Lonely Hearts Club Band.* You can find him in the second row, between beat movement icon and writer William Burroughs and the comedy legend Stan Laurel. From the deep mystery of existence, to the cover of a pop-culture ground-breaking work of art—such is the fate of invisible-visible master Mahavatar Babaji.

❋

Like Bodhisattva, Sage, Saint, Yogi(ni), and Tantrik(a), Avatar is one of the spiritual archetypes that can be utilized on the spiritual path. It may be the one most appropriate for our age, given that, as a species, we need to rethink and reinvent who we are and to create the next level of human evolution rather than collapse into old patterns and regressive tendencies.

Avatar simply means "descent" in Sanskrit and designates a special being that descended from the Divine realms into the human dimension with a clear plan on how to reduce ignorance and suffering and bring human spiritual evolution to the next level. The most notable avatars in our spiritual history are Krishna, Christ and Buddha. While avatars usually depart from the Earth as soon as their mission is accomplished, mahavatars or great avatars, help and guide a slower evolutionary progress which may last for centuries. That is what makes Mahavatar Babaji so special and important.

❋

Imagine you can remember your past lives, just the way you remember your life three or five years ago. That's what avatars do.

❋

# Spirit X

And—Yes!—some beings incarnate into human form just to bring the Dharma to the next level. Says Krishna in the *Bhagavad Gita*: "To protect the righteous, to disintegrate the dark forces, to establish the Dharma, I am born from age to age."

❦

Mahavatar Babaji knows and lives the secret of secrets: from Nothingness, Everything is created. As such, he is the master of disappearing and appearing. And as an Avatar, he is the master of descending and ascending. As Everything-That-Is-Nothing and one who is So-Far-And-So-Close, Babaji masters both dimensions of Spirit, unmanifest and manifest. Like a magician, he lives in the dimensions of both pure Spirit and evolutionary Creation. As an Avatar, he masters descending (Spirit emptying itself into form all the way to matter) and ascending (Spirit finding its way Home from matter to spirit through evolutionary growth). It is this ascending evolutionary blueprint that is the real gift of Babaji to humankind at this point of human evolution.

❦

Have you seen Babaji's eyes? Awe… The depth beyond existence.

Have you seen Babaji's hair? Awe… The pregnant Void beyond space-time.

## The Way of Mahavatar Babaji

❁

In accordance with Babaji's being, the Way of Mahavatar Babaji is the mastery of disappearing-appearing and ascending-descending. Both disappearing-appearing and ascending-descending should be taken here in the sense of human dimension and not necessarily as the qualities of spiritual Avatar. What would be spiritual disappearing at this point of human evolution? It is letting go of ego-identification, transcendence (and inclusion) of your ego. How many times we have heard in spiritual circles that if you really want some things to happen to you or if you want some real results—you need to get out of the way. Meaning: disappear, let go of ego-identification, let Reality take care of it.

❁

In deep dreamless sleep, you truly disappear.

❁

Take a walk in nature—and disappear.
Make love to your Beloved—and disappear.
Listen to your favorite song—and disappear.
Meditate—and disappear.
Go to sleep—and disappear.
Be—and disappear.

❁

# Spirit X

Genuine disappearance of ego is actually a full tasting of Reality—by being Reality. So, paradoxically, when you disappear as ego, you appear as Reality and its many qualities such as Clarity, Peace, Love, Flow, etc. Appearing in the Way of Mahavatar Babaji is nothing but shining a pure Light in the body-mind-world, showing up in the body-mind-world fully and freely, embodying a taste of Reality beyond ego-identification.

❊

Dear friend, stop reading this book for a few minutes: Disappear…

Welcome back. Appear—Show Up! Thanks.

❊

The Ascending-Descending module within the Way of Mahavatar Babaji is based on a simple fact regarding the fabric of the human dimension and the universe itself. Whether you realize it or not, human life is growth, an evolution. If this growth is done properly, one will taste and embody higher and wider Insight, Love, Connectivity, Productivity, Purpose and Ease all the way to our Divinity. This multi-growth potential structure is inherent to the fabric of the universe (movement from matter to life to mind to soul to Spirit) and it is up to us-humans (evolutionary we-the-people) to recognize, activate, and co-create with the Divine. So, whether you realize it or not, we are spiritually ascending during our lifetimes. In the Way of Mahavatar Babaji we will utilize simple techniques of spiritual ascending and descending.

❦

Here is a simple practice for spiritual Ascending-Descending.

Sit in a comfortable position
Re-lax
Close your eyes
Envision in your mind's eye a shining White Light
Simply surrender to it.
Now visualize the same White Light
Just a bit above your head
Bring your attention to the White Light
Through your crown chakra.
Acknowledge Ascending
Stay with that White Light above your crown chakra
Surrender to it
And soak up its qualities.
Now descend
Simply bring the White Light
Into your mind-body
And offer it to the world
Moment-to-moment.
Re-member the White Light
By embodying it
And offering it to the others and the world.

❦

# Spirit X

Here is another example of what might be called everyday Ascending-Descending. We have already noticed that human life can be seen as growth through various stages (as long as the growth is done properly, without regression or too many pathologies). According to that view, adults are more developed spiritually—and in other capacities—than children. So, you have already ascended to a certain stage. Now, learn how to descend to the children's level. Say, make an attempt to explain to 3-5 year old children some of your life-changing spiritual experiences. Descend into their world and their hearts. Use appropriate language (Spirit-Land instead of Awareness, angels instead of archetypes), gestures and vibrations to make your point. Notice evolutionary descending in the process. The purpose of this exercise and example is to point to the fact that some basic levels of Ascending and Descending are already happening in our everyday lives.

❁

Another powerful and productive practice that can be developed within the Way of Mahavatar Babaji is deity yoga. As a matter of fact, in Spirit X we recommend deity yoga whenever we practice with deities. Deity yoga as a practice can be found, in one form or another, in numerous wisdom traditions, with its fullest and highest development in Tantric Buddhism. In Spirit X, deity yoga is the movement from 2nd person visualization-meditation on a deity to 1st person identification with the deity, which leads to Realization and embodiment.

# The Way of Mahavatar Babaji

In Spirit X we distinguish three stages of deity yoga: visualization-meditation, merging-Realization and embodiment. One starts deity yoga by choosing a deity or being chosen by a deity. The step that may help the visualization-meditation stage is enriching one's environment with images and statues of the deity (very easy to find in present day global world). Visualization-meditation is the practice of visualizing the deity in one's mind's eye with the focus on the distinguished qualities of particular deity (for instance, self-transcending love for Jesus, compassion for Kuan Yin, or creative energy for Shakti). Also, visualization-meditation should open the space for any kind of energy and vibration exchange between the deity and practitioner. In general, deities should be approached as subtle beings willing to help us in terns of healing, spiritual realization and evolution of consciousness. This first stage of deity yoga is done in the 2nd person fashion: there is meditating subject (practitioner) meditating upon divine object (deity).

The second stage of deity yoga is crucial and should be done only by advanced practitioners. In the second stage, practitioner and deity merge in the divine union and release their togetherness into pure awareness, which is nothing but the True Self common to everyone and everything. Merging is done by bringing the deity into one's Heart. At this sub-stage of the second stage, one can visualize himself or herself as the deity. After the merging stage, one realizes that merging itself happened on the ground of the empty and luminous nature of the practitioner's self and the deity's self, after which Realization of the True Self takes place. Together with the deity into your and everyone's True Self —that is the essence of deity yoga. After the realization of emptiness and luminosity of the True Self, one re-embraces the body-mind-world and helps others do the same by embodying the major qualities of the deity.

❁

Deity yoga is an advanced practice and is not for everyone. Actually, the first stage of deity yoga, visualization-meditation with the emphasis on receiving certain qualities from the deity, is recommended to a wide spectrum of practitioners. However, the second and third stage is recommended only to advanced practitioners, with a solid understanding of the empty and luminous nature of the True Self. Without this spiritual understanding, deity yoga can become a dangerous case of ego-inflation (dangerous for practitioners themselves, others and the world). Nothing is more spiritually dangerous than egos that imagine that they are gods. However, a fair realization of the True Self is a guarantee that the practitioner is not going to fall into the trap of ego-inflation.

❁

If you resonate with the Babaji archetype or are chosen by Babaji for spiritual help and a mission, here are some suggestions on how to do deity yoga with Babaji. Start by choosing some images and statues of Babaji and give them a special place in your everyday environment. As of visualization-meditation, visualize Babaji in your mind's eye. Pay attention visually to all the details. Be open in terms of what you feel and what you hear, since deities can communicate with us via images, feelings or voice/thoughts. Stay open. Pay particular attention to the distinguished qualities of Mahavatar Babaji, such as Immortality, Power, Clarity, Love, Translucency, Beauty, Understanding of Cosmic Evolution, Supreme Realization, and East-West Integration. After practicing visualization-meditation for a while, either initiate merging with the deity or allow the merging to happen on its own when the time is ripe. Merging happens by simply bringing the deity into your Heart. Yes, bring Babaji into your Heart. To help the process, you can even visualize yourself as Babaji, since essentially your identity and the deity's entity are one and the same. If you stay with the process of merging or visualizing yourself as the deity—the realization of the empty and luminous nature of your and everyone's True Self will happen. Rest as luminous emptiness, pure awareness. Taste fully your True Self, and thank Babaji for that. After practicing Realization, pay particular attention to embodying some awakened qualities of Mahavatar Babaji (Power, Translucency, Evolution, Realization, etc.). Deity yoga is a superb mode of practice, Realization and expression.

This universe is haloed by Babaji.

All the universes are haloed by Babaji.

# Spirit X

❊

In terms of the three-part structure of the Ways, the Way of Mahavatar Babaji unfolds in the following fashion. At the practice-seeking stage the best practice to utilize is visualization-meditation on Babaji, supported by creating an environment that supports and resembles this Way. At this stage the practice of ascending-descending can be useful. As for Realization, the practices of disappearing-appearing and the second stage of deity yoga are recommended. As for Service-Expression, the key is to embody, moment-to-moment, the awakened qualities of Babaji, such as Immortality, Power, Spiritual Evolution, Beauty, Translucency and East-West Integration. The Way of Mahavatar Babaji is mostly for practitioners passionate about East-West integration and the evolution of consciousness, since that is the core of Babaji's mission in the human dimension.

❊

"There is no separation for us, my beloved child. Wherever you are, wherever you call me, I shall be with you instantly."—Babaji to Lahiri Mahasaya.

❊

Practices and modules that support the Way of Mahavatar Babaji are meditation, inquiry, silence, satsang and body-mind-spirit cross-training.

# The Way of Mahavatar Babaji

❋

From Eternity to Eternity—Babaji.

From Eternity to Eternity—You.

Spirit X

#44

# The Way of Shiva

The Way of Shiva is another Spirit X Way of Liberation and Expression with and through an archetypal deity. Alongside with Jesus on the Cross and meditating Buddha, Shiva—in its many forms—is one of the most famous symbols and most powerful archetypes in world spirituality. For the purposes of Spirit X, we will utilize a three-part essence of Shiva. In Hindu mythology, religion, spirituality and culture, Shiva is depicted as a mountain yogi, a lover-householder and a cosmic dancer. Shiva's pure form is a mountain yogi and his absolute full expressions are partner-family man and cosmic dancer.

Shiva is a Mahayogi, a supreme yogi. If Babaji is the teacher of teachers, Shiva is the yogi of yogis. Shiva mountain yogi is depicted in a sitting meditation posture with eyes closed. He is gray like ash, indicating that he is beyond the cycles of life and death, creation and destruction. As such he is the Lord of Transformation. He is, also, free from the world since the world is his dream. He is ascetic, free from desire, and thus at peace, which is very visible on his peaceful-blissful face. The symbol and archetype of Shiva mountain yogi is powerful and essential since it indicates that Shiva's absorption in himself is his full absorption with

# The Way of Shiva

Ultimate Reality. Shiva's Atman (individual essence) is identical to Brahman (the essence of Reality). Just as your Atman is identical to Brahman. Essential, straightforward, plain and simple: going within is the ultimate way to Freedom and Self-Realization. And, plain and simple: Shiva is the Lord of Transformation and Liberation.

Inhale, exhale
Inhale, exhale
Notice the space between the two breaths
That's where Shiva the mountain yogi abides
That's where you are One with Shiva
Beyond breath
Beyond birth and death
Beyond creation and destruction.

White-grey ashes
In the dark empty space
Remains of destruction
Seeds of creation
SHIVA

Have you seen the Adiyogi Shiva statue in Coimbatore, India designed by Sadhguru Jaggi Vasudev and the Isha Foundation? Awe... It is the largest bust sculpture in the world. When quantity and quality meet in out-of-this world vibration. Awe…

Shiva mountain yogi is an empty Shiva, Shiva's essence before his full manifestation and dance. Shiva mountain yogi is always depicted with a yogic, strong and athletic body, which means that he is always ready for the tantric embrace of Parvati-Shakti and the whole universe. Thus his full expression is either Shiva lover-householder or Shiva cosmic dancer.

As a lover Shiva is usually depicted in polarity-unity with Shakti and as a lover and family man he is depicted with his wife Parvati and their sons Ganesha and Karttikeya. In the Shiva-Shakti polarity-unity, Shiva is consciousness and Shakti is the cosmic energy-power. Shiva-Shakti polarity-unity is still the best way to understand and embody the masculine and feminine principles from a spiritual standpoint. Both Shiva and Shakti need each other. Shiva needs Shakti to get embodied and to move, and Shakti needs Shiva to get awakened, activated and for a sense of direction. Shiva-Shakti polarity-unity is a superb way to connect human condition (whether man or woman) with the higher cosmic principles and energies all the way to the One and spiritual Enlightenment.

# The Way of Shiva

As a partner, lover and father, Shiva is also depicted in unity with Parvati (a particular manifestation of the universal Shakti). The Hindu myth about how Shiva and Parvati met and created divine unity certainly has a spiritual significance. According to the myth, Vishnu, the God Creator, noticed that Shiva, one of the three cosmic rulers, was not fulfilling his Dharma. Shiva, the great destroyer—and yes, destruction is needed in cosmic process for new things to emerge—is engaged in deep meditation instead of fulfilling his cosmic duty. Vishnu comes up with a plan to re-engage Shiva in the cosmic process by sending the Goddess manifestation in the human realm. Parvati is young and naive yet beautiful and seductive having the qualities of a divine Muse. After realizing that awakening Shiva's desire for her is not enough to fully engage him in the cosmic process (including her), Parvati pulls out the last resource to win Shiva's heart: she wholeheartedly engages in deep and genuine yoga. It is her deep practice, devotion and radiance that finally bring Shiva to Earth. He is now a lover, devoted father and family man and, on top of that, he fulfills his cosmic duty.

The spiritual significance of this story is enormous. It reminds us that the spiritual journey does not necessarily need to be a hero's quest—like in the cases of Buddha or Jesus—but can also be a relational and even family affair. Enlightenment in the world is possible—moreover, it is its highest expression. Now is the time to utilize this Shiva's practical wisdom. For centuries, the most dominant form of spirituality was an ascetic one. One withdraws from the world in order to find Liberation and the True Self. For centuries sex, relationships and family have been considered to be obstacles on the path. Shiva's and Parvati's tantric household is an invitation for us as practitioners to resolve the biggest duality in spiritual history (certainly embodied in the Shiva archetype): the duality between ascetic yogi and the householder. There is no more appropriate spiritual wisdom for our time than this one. We live in times of integration and spiritually that means a genuine marriage of Spirit and Form, Spirit and Life.

What did you do today to integrate Spirit and Life, internally or externally? Individually or collectively?

Shiva and Parvati are tantric lovers. After their wedding, they go together to Mount Kailash and make love for eons on clouds and mountaintops, in the subtle, high-vibrational realm. Shiva's tantra, actually, rests upon three basic principles: 1) pleasure is a way to the Bliss of Being and Liberation, 2) embracing opposites and going beyond them is a way to Bliss and Liberation, 3) kundalini yoga is a way to Bliss and Liberation.

Pleasure in the human realm is nothing but an echo of the Bliss of Being. As such, it can be utilized as a vehicle for re-discovery of primordial Unity and Bliss, the goal of

# The Way of Shiva

Tantra. Instead of rejecting pleasure, or getting wrapped up into it, one—with the help of Buddha, Dharma and Sangha—uses food, touch, sex, music, material wealth, arts, dance, and much more as a means for expanding, ego-transcendence and Awakening.

Tantra as the practice of embracing opposites and going Beyond may be one of the most efficient tricks on the spiritual path. As long as we strive for positive phenomena and experiences and reject the negative ones, we are playing a spiritually inefficient game of picking and choosing. Pain, failures, sickness, old age, death, crisis, war and disasters are part of Shiva's play and rejecting them means rejecting the fullness of Reality and… your Liberation and True Self. Shiva's radical tantra of accepting full reality beyond opposites, paradoxically reveals to us the primordial Unity and the Bliss of Being.

Shiva archetype is portrayed with many symbols around him, cobra being one of the most distinctive ones. It represents the kundalini serpent, which is, in the human microcosm, the energy coiled and dormant in the base of the spine. Once awakened with spiritual practice, this energy ascends through the chakras (energy centers-levels) culminating in spiritual awakening in the crown chakra, where the kundalini energy meets pure consciousness. Kundalini yoga is one of the most confusing and polluted fields in contemporary spirituality, and we suggest kundalini yoga only to practitioners who have cleared their subtle-energy channels and work with qualified and trusted kundalini yoga teachers and groups.

# Spirit X

Shiva's biggest dilemma and hesitation: Why enter manifestation? Yet, he knows it: to be not only Free, but also Full. And for that, he needs Parvati-Shakti and the world.

Shiva is ultimately hip: bad boy deity, post-conventional archetype, never fully domesticated, Mahayogi beyond creation and destruction.

Parvati is ultimately hip: seductive Goddess, tantric lover, mother, Muse, Yogini.

Another way for Shiva to fully manifest is to become the Cosmic Dancer. This time Shiva the Mountain Yogi is embracing the whole universe. Shiva Cosmic Dancer is perhaps the most potent and powerful symbol in the whole of world spirituality. He is depicted as Nataraja, the Lord of Dance, dancing within the circle of fire representing space-time and manifestation. As with the mountain yogi, his face is peaceful and blissful. His beautiful yogic hair extends to all corners of the universe, representing that he knows everything because he is everything. He has four arms, his upper right arm holding the drum that puts creation into existence via primordial drumbeat-vibration. His lower

# The Way of Shiva

right hand is lifted up and open signaling: "Be not afraid, in spite of how things may look, everything is all right." His lower left hand points to his feet, left one smashing the repulsive and ignorant ego-dwarf, caught up into a heavy cycle of samsara. Shiva's right foot is raised, representing spiritual lightness, non-attachment and complete freedom from manifestation. The symbol of the Dancing Shiva points to the fullness of manifestation and the freedom of the ultimate-unmanifest—and, Shiva's omnipresence and omnipotence in both realms (which are ultimately One).

Dancing Shiva is total movement in pure stillness, total fullness and total freedom.

In all of its richness, glory and beauty, the two aspects of the Dancing Shiva symbol and archetype are of crucial importance for Spirit X. Shiva pressing the ego-dwarf points to the necessity of ego-transcendence in spiritual life and spiritual evolution. Humans develop from pre-ego to ego to trans-ego. Although pre-egoic and egoic identification are a natural part of the human condition and evolution—transcending ego is the cornerstone of adult spiritual life. That's why Shiva takes no prisoners: you either transcend ego through effort and practice or Life-Shiva destroys ego with fierce grace. There is a deep wisdom in ego-transcendence since only fleeting freedom and happiness are available to ego-identification. The ego-dwarf keeps falling down again and again.

Another crucial aspect of the Dancing Shiva, which speaks to our age, is his raised foot. It is a reminder and pointer to the lightness of being and to our (and the world's) unmanifest, pure essence. Genuine spiritual practice is always either glimpsing or abiding as pure consciousness—Nothing which is Everything, the Isness. In the age when the world of form is transforming at accelerating speed, ego cannot help but get confused and overwhelmed by it—thus getting in touch with our unmanifest, pure essence becomes a necessity. Dancing Shiva is an extraordinary symbol of Eternity-Infinity and, indeed, a spiritual medicine for what needs to be done in our time.

How is your ego-dwarf today?

Like with all the archetypes and deities in Spirit X, we strongly recommend doing deity yoga with the Shiva archetype if a practitioner feels drawn to this archetype or the archetype comes to the practitioner. We have already mentioned a three-part structure of deity yoga in Spirit X: 1) visualization-meditation, 2) merging-Realization, 3) embodiment. Start deity yoga with the Shiva archetype by enriching your environment with Shiva and by visualizing Shiva in your mind's eye in regular meditations. In terms of his multiple forms, Shiva is one of the richest archetypes in

# The Way of Shiva

world spirituality. Thus, you can visualize Shiva the mountain yogi, or Shiva tantric lover, or Shiva householder, or Shiva the Cosmic Dancer. Simply visualize Shiva in a chosen form with emphasis on the particular qualities of that Shiva form. For instance, for the Shiva the mountain yogi, focus on the qualities of beyond-worldliness, peace and freedom from desire. For Shiva tantric lover, focus on the holiness of pleasure, tantra beyond opposites and kundalini energy.

The second stage of merging-Realization can be initiated or allowed to happen spontaneously. If you want to initiate merging with Shiva, simply bring the Shiva archetype into your Heart and let the magic of merging and disappearing together into Source happen. You can also visualize yourself as Shiva—in the chosen form—but, please, don't make deity yoga a case of ego-inflation. While in divine union with Shiva, notice that union happens due to the space in which everything happens (arises-shines-dissolves). Or, merge with Shiva so fully that you both get released into the empty open space. Be that space. Be That. Be Yourself. Make sure that you are capable of coming back to that space of your True Self at your will. After you become familiar with Realization, bring it step forward in terms of expression, with the focus on embodying the numerous qualities of the Shiva archetype such as Peace, Bliss, tantric lovemaking, tantric householder, cosmic dancer-embracer, and much more. Thank Shiva for his guidance and help, and be grateful that you have enriched your world with the subtle realm and subtle archetypes.

# Spirit X

Again, deity yoga is not for everyone. We recommend it only for advanced practitioners, those ones with a decent understanding of emptiness. Don't make your spiritual life a case of ego-inflation, full of arrogance and ignorance.

In terms of three-part structure of the Ways (practice-seeking, Realization, Service-Expression), the Way of Shiva is one of the richest ones. The Shiva practitioner designs a Shiva oriented spiritual practice that includes meditating on Shiva or emptiness, tantric sex, a tantric relationship to Life and Reality, Shiva-inspired yoga, dance and much more. One of the advantages of the Shiva archetype is that it is very vast, which gives practitioner many ways to practice.

As for Realization, the second stage of deity yoga (merging with the deity) is recommended, as well as many other practices such as resting as non-desiring Peace, sexual or total Tantra, radical embrace of opposites, resting beyond birth and death and beyond creation and destruction, being the nondual dance of the universe, etc. The Shiva-Realizer simply feels comfortable and at peace in every moment and every situation, and lives the dance of emptiness and form, consciousness and energy.

When it comes to the Service-Expression stage of the Way of Shiva, one has many options to live a Shiva-like awakened life. One can express the Peace and Bliss of Being,

## The Way of Shiva

serve as an awakened householder, express awakened lover or cosmic dancer, embody the yogi-alchemist, and many more. As we said earlier, the Shiva archetype is one of the most powerful in world spirituality and certainly one that is most applicable to our age of accelerating transformation.

Listen… Listen deeply… Can you hear the Sound of Shiva's drum, calling you to Awaken.

Listen… Listen deeply… Can you hear the Sound of Shiva's drum, calling you to march as Spirit on Earth.

Open… Open fully… Can you feel the Vibration of Shiva's drum, creating the cosmic game, expanding Shakti into Infinity, creating myriad forms and names.

My friend, Shiva's dance is in your heart, as the Bliss of Being—Ananda.

Have you seen the Dancing Shiva statue in front of the European Organization for Nuclear Research (CERN) in Geneva, Switzerland: Shiva uniting Art, Science and Spirituality and integrating East and West. Awe…

# Spirit X

After all, Shiva in Sanskrit means "the auspicious one." He knows and embodies the secret: Bliss is prior to suffering, bliss is stronger than suffering.

Shiva's hand is raised and open: It's all OK.

Shiva's foot is raised: beyond gravity, beyond space-time, beyond manifestation.

Practices and modules that support the Way of Shiva are meditation, prayer, kirtan, yoga, movement, dance, silence, relationships, sex, technology, body-mind-spirit cross training, arts and many more.

Om Namah Shivaja.

#45

# The Way of Madonna, the Holy Mother

The Way of Madonna, the Holy Mother is another Spirit X Way of Liberation and Expression which utilizes an archetypal deity, this time from the Christian religious and spiritual tradition. Madonna with child is the embodiment and emanation of pure Spirit, relational and unitive Love and saintly Light. Many other names for Madonna are Holy Mother, God-bearer, Virgin Mary, and St. Mary. In the Spirit X teaching we choose Madonna since she is almost always depicted with child in her arms, thus pointing to Love in both its dualistic-relational and nondual-unitive forms, which is the core of Christianity as both a religion and spiritual teaching.

☾✝

The mythic narrative is not without its spiritual significance: Mary was an ordinary young Jewish woman married to Joseph, until angel Gabriel visited her and told her that she was to be the mother of a Messiah (Christ), the Son of God. Mary conceived with the Holy Spirit and took her fate with extraordinary faith, courage and responsibility. Baby Jesus was born in a stable in Bethlehem, surrounded by animals. The rest is History, the history of Christianity, the history of the Western world and, indeed, the history of our global age. For both believers and non-believers, Christianity stays as one of the basic frameworks for understanding the human condition and the universe.

☪✝

The spiritual and archetypal significance of Madonna rests upon three principles: virgin birth, motherhood and saintly Light. Virgin birth points to the purity of Spirit, motherhood activates Love in both the relational and unitive forms, and if motherhood is complemented with a spiritual practice and life, it can produce saintly qualities within the human dimension.

☪✝

The virgin birth has been a subject for a lot of doctrines, cultural values, religious and moral fanaticism, misunderstandings and mockery. Religious believers take it literally and consider it to be one of the foundation stones of the Christian doctrine, traditional people make it a cultural norm, secular humanists and atheists take it as mythic nonsense, and modern people do not know how to incorporate it into their modern lives. One way or another, Madonna's virgin birth has survived centuries and, thus in Spirit X we take the opportunity to utilize it spiritually. From a spiritual perspective the virgin birth is a metaphor for the purity of Spirit. If Jesus is Christ-Messiah and the Son of God, he must be the expression and embodiment of pure Spirit. That's why he doesn't have human parents and is not conceived through human intercourse. On the other hand, there must be something in Mary-Madonna that matches Jesus' purity—thus virgin birth. Virgin birth is simply how mythic mind interprets and expresses pure Spirit in the human form.

☽✝

Pure spirit in the human form? Sounds familiar? Have you heard this description and pointer already? Isn't this your innermost intuition about who you are and about Life in general? And isn't that exactly what needs to be done spiritually in our times? And from there, pours into all other areas of our life and dimensions of cosmos?

☽✝

A spiritual practice and life can be seen as a re-awakening of primordial virginity: we peel off the layers of human contamination until we re-discover the primordial virginity of pure Spirit within us. That which is untouched by anything in the human dimension. Stabilizing in that virginity and finding creative ways to express it in human form and world brings about a free and full spiritual life in our age. So, it is important to differentiate between spiritual virginity and a biological and moral one.

☽✝

Have you seen the *Sistine Madonna* by Raphael, one of the most famous paintings of Madonna? Marriage of religion and Renaissance art, motherly love and caring embrace, saintly Luminosity, innocence of a child, revelation of the Divine. Awe... Just Awe...

☾✝

Madonna is a metaphor and expression of motherly love, partly within this world, partly out of this world. Madonna is by definition portrayed with the child, baby Jesus, in her arms. The spiritual message is clear here: Madonna and baby Jesus are two-in-One. Madonna is in the relationship of motherly love with her baby and, simultaneously, she is the expression of pure Love and pure Spirit. Love as relationship and love as unity—the true gift of Christianity. If Jesus is the embodiment of Spirit that leads to Love (me and God as ultimately One), Madonna is the embodiment of Love that leads to Spirit (me and child as two-in-One).

☾✝

Close your eyes
Envision that you hold a child in your arms
It can be a child dear to you, or a child that came straight from Spirit
Feel the embrace
Feel Love as a relationship and an embrace
Be that Love
Investigate into Love as a relationship
And let the relationship dissolve into Unity
A non-separation between you and the child
Be that Love, too.

# The Way of Madonna, the Holy Mother

Investigate into that divine Embrace and Unity.
What is the space in which it happens
What is the space that makes it possible
Be that space
Be that spaceless space
Repeat the meditation by envisioning the globe
Instead of the child.
Repeat meditation by envisioning various phenomena
As objects of divine Embrace and Union.
Use meditation as a vehicle for the discovery of Divine Unity
Which is nothing but your True Self.
Be Love
Pure Love.

☾✝

Love is a relationship, you and me becoming Whole through each other.

Love is a relationship with God. What is God, if you cannot be in relationship with Him? God in the second person, as the Great Thou, the Beloved—the ultimate gift of Christianity.

Love is embrace. Me and you merging together and moving from two to One.

Love is an offering that doesn't require anything in return. Love is an offering that finds fulfillment in the very act of offering. Love is selfless.

# Spirit X

Love is pouring yourself into the world, fully, passionately, boldly. This pouring activates the endless nectar of Love that you are. The more you do it, the more you activate the nectar.

Love is the stateless state of non-separation, of being Whole, of Unity. What is God, if you cannot be one with Him? Your essence as identical to God's, God as the absolute Self—the ultimate gift of many wisdom traditions.

Be this spectrum of Love.

Be Love.

☾✝

Whenever you give yourself fully—that is Love. What an easy practice, what a great life.

☾✝

Jesus is the biggest archetype in world history, although heavily misinterpreted and misused, spiritually and energetically polluted. Nevertheless, there is no more important archetype. What is extraordinary, unique and beautifully simple about Jesus is that he is a pure example of embodied spirituality. He was and is a living embodiment of pure Spirit. At every occasion, he removed ignorance and separation. He didn't necessarily teach, he didn't leave any teachings, books or written records, he simply lived it. He lived That. He lived pure spirit in human form. If Jesus is embodied Spirit (me and Spirit as One), Madonna is Embodied Love (me and you as two-in-One).

☾✝

The last principle of the Madonna archetype is saintly Light. In the Christian tradition, saints are persons who lived life of extraordinary faith, moral virtue and devotion to God. They often portray some heroic characteristics such as piety, humility and courage. The vast majority of saints are venerated after death. From a spiritual standpoint, saints demonstrate some type of holiness in secular life. They are usually depicted with a halo around their head, indicating that they are an expression of Divine Light and Grace. They are, also, capable of illumining that Light to others. So, spiritually, saints are connected to and are an expression of Divine Light.

Madonna, the Holy Mother, is the expression of Divine Light through her connection to pure Spirit and the virtues of motherhood. The truth is, this saintly Light can be awaken through spiritual practice, devotion to God and acts of service. We live in times when many higher religious and spiritual types across many wisdom traditions such as saint, yogi(ni), sage, bodhisattva, avatar, tantrik(a), are available to practitioners in the global world. As human and cosmic evolution accelerates, we need more saintly Light to guide us and support us.

☾✝

# Spirit X

Awaken the Madonna saintly Light by lovingly embracing yourself, others, the world and the Divine.

☾ †

Like with other archetypes, we recommend the practice of deity yoga with Madonna, the Holy Mother. Start by choosing some images and statues of Madonna and give them a special place in your environment. Give them regular attention. As for the first stage of deity yoga (visualization-meditation), visualize Madonna with child in your mind's eye. Feel the divine Love and Embrace between Madonna and baby Jesus and recognize the purity of Spirit as the background upon which the embrace is happening. Be open to what you see, hear or feel (since seeing, hearing or feeling are major mediums of this stage of deity yoga).

Initiate the second stage of deity yoga (merging-Realization) by either bringing Madonna into your Heart or by allowing the merging to happen spontaneously as a result of regular and open-hearted visualization-meditation. If it helps, you can visualize yourself as Madonna (no ego-inflation, please). Allow a complete merging with Madonna, and release that togetherness into the pure Spirit of your and everyone's True Self. Taste fully and stabilize as your True Self.

After stabilizing Realization, embody and express to others and the world the awakened qualities of the Madonna archetype such as relational and unitive Love, divine Embrace and pure Spirit. Thank Madonna for her help and guidance, and be grateful that you expanded your world and opened a regular access to the subtle world of archetypes.

☾†

The Way of Madonna, the Holy Mother, is the way of liberation and expression through Love, Embrace and purity of Spirit. In terms of three-part structure of the Ways (practice-seeking, Realization, Service-Expression), the Way of Madonna, unfolds in the following fashion. The Madonna inspired practitioner meditates upon Madonna, and utilizes Love and Embrace in both practice and life. Love your family, partner, friends, nation, globe and the cosmos. Embrace your family, partner, friends, world and the Divine. Practice and live love as a relationship. Also, the practitioner at this stage can utilize the purity (of Spirit) in many dimensions of our being. What does it mean to eat pure food? How is it to be in pure relationship? How is a life of integrity connected to a life of pure Spirit? Inquiries like this can really propel one towards Self-Realization.

As for the second stage of the Way of Madonna, Realization, the second stage of the deity yoga is recommended as well as radical, unconditional Love and Embrace. Also, practices that reveal to us pure Spirit—such as nondual meditation and inquiry—are recommended. The key at this stage is to practice and live love as unity. The Madonna-Realizer is the embodiment of pure Love, Embrace and Spirit, moment-to-moment. In a world of polarization and fragmentation—one of the biggest challenges of our time—Madonna's Love and Embrace is a true gift and medicine.

# Spirit X

☾†

Practices and modules that support the Way of Madonna are meditation, prayer, inquiry, silence, kirtan, relationships, connecting with others and the arts.

☾†

Have you seen Raphael's *Sistine Madonna*?... Have you felt Madonna in your Heart?... Have you embraced the world with your Heart?

#46

# THE WAY OF WILBER

Ken Wilber is one of the rare modern and contemporary philosophers who acknowledges spirituality. Moreover, his contribution to redefining and updating both spirituality and Enlightenment has been unparalleled in modern times. Although his integral spirituality is still evolving—being routed in both timeless and spaceless unmanifest Spirit and ever-evolving manifest Spirit—its latest version includes four areas of spirituality: Waking Up, Growing Up, Cleaning Up and Showing Up. Although Cleaning Up (bringing unconscious and repressed psychological material to the light of awareness) and Showing Up (using the Integral map to show up in the world fully, wholly and maturely) are important in spirituality, our main focus in this book will be on the Waking Up and Growing Up teachings, since this is where Wilber's contribution to the wisdom traditions and present day spirituality is crucial.

Wilber is aware of both the good news and the bad news when in comes to spirituality in our age. On the one hand, we live in extraordinary times: wisdom, teachings, and skillful means from all the wisdom traditions are easily available to us in our global and digital world. Also, more practitioners worldwide are becoming genuinely interested in spirituality. On the other hand, the bad news regarding spirituality is that spirituality and Enlightenment are still unrecognized by the vast majority of humans, theories and institutions on this planet. Enlightenment, Awakening, Liberation or re-discovery of the True Self is literally the most precious jewel we have cultivated on this planet and in the human dimension—and, yet, the very possibility of total Liberation and realization of the True Self is not on our cultural, educational and psychological maps. In that respect, Wilber is a true Warrior of genuine Spirit.

Wilber devoted a great deal of his life to updating the Dharma. Drawing from the best systems and teachings from both East and West, he has made an attempt to reintroduce spirituality in modern and postmodern world.

His biggest contribution to the wisdom traditions, and spirituality in general, is a discovery that spiritual development actually happens in two developmental spectrums, both in spirit and in mind, or, as he puts it, via state-stages (Waking Up) and via structure-stages (Growing Up). Many genuine spiritual systems focus on the development of the states of consciousness (spiritual technologies of consciousness transformation) and the vast majority of present day religions are actually expressions of development (or not) of structures of consciousness (belief in certain narrative and dogma). No spiritual or religious system combines both. Spirituality of the present-day and future, Wilber argues, should definitely include both of the spectrums in their teachings. Also, wisdom traditions should update their teachings since the world has evolved since their emergence.

State-stages follow the development of one's identity from ego to True Self. Wilber is using the developmental state model from Vedanta Hinduism that recognizes five major states of consciousness: gross, subtle, causal, witnessing and nondual (relying on the three natural states of consciousness: waking, dreaming and deep dreamless sleep).

The gross state of consciousness is the most familiar to the vast majority of people in the present day world: it is ordinary, waking consciousness, characterized by subject-object dualism and ego-identification. (In the present day world, the most people's attention is actually stuck in this state-stage). The subtle state of consciousness is available in dreaming, daydreaming, visualizations, states of creative flow and visions. The causal state of consciousness is available in deep dreamless sleep and formless meditation. Witnessing is a capacity of unbroken attention though all three previous states of consciousness. Nondual awareness is actually not a state of consciousness but ever-present ground of all states in which the last remains of subject-object division are finally resolved.

The nature of states of consciousness is that they come

and go; however, with spiritual practice and, especially states-training, states of consciousness can be transformed into permanent traits. "Converting temporary states into permanent traits" is one of the early mottos of Wilber's integral spirituality. With transforming states of consciousness into permanent traits, one's identity moves from ego (gross) to soul (subtle) to True Self (witnessing and nondual).

Waking Up teachings about the development via states of consciousness are the only explicit vehicle to ultimate Liberation and Self-Realization. In that respect, they are a real treasure and deserve to be preserved so that we don't lose touch with them in our busy, fast and overwhelming world. They also need to be updated so that they can resonate with global modern individuals. Both Integral Theory and Spirit X offer this update.

Another treasure when it comes to states of consciousness is that they open access to the various realms of Being. To each state—gross, subtle or causal—there is a corresponding realm that opens with it. So part of spiritual training for integral practitioners in the Way of Wilber is to cultivate access to the various realms of Being via mastering states of consciousness.

One of the major problems on this planet, from a spiritual standpoint, is that the vast majority of people are stuck in the gross realm—characterized by various forms of duality (I–world, me–you, us–them), ego-identification (which itself brings quite an amount of suffering), and various forms of materialism (which provide only fleeting happiness and further feed into the cycle of it's-never-enough type of suffering). Mastering states of consciousness and accessing realms of Being other than the gross one, will open us individually and collectively to more energetic and subtle aspects of ourselves and Reality and indeed accelerate and enhance the necessary process of ego-transcendence.

Natural states of consciousness are a gift inherent to the human condition. Being a human means that you wake, dream and sleep. Buddhas wake, dream and sleep, babies wake, dream and sleep and serial killers wake, dream and sleep. It is Wilber's legacy to have reintroduced this jewel into the modern and post-modern world and it is up to us, the practitioners, to utilize it and inspire others to do the same. Natural and trained states of consciousness are one of the keys for further spiritual evolution on this planet. It is incredible how much transformation—and Awakening, indeed—can be accomplished just by re-directing our attention. What a relief…

Structure-stages follow the development of one's relative self into ever-increasing complexity, evolutionary depth, connectivity and meaning. In his structure-stages teaching

# Spirit X

Wilber mostly uses Swiss anthropologist Gebser's developmental worldview model: from archaic to magic to mythic to rational to pluralistic to integral. The structure-stages part of Wilber's integral spirituality is vital for understanding and embodying the evolving part of the Dharma (Growing Up). Spiritual Enlightenment—and any genuine spiritual experience for that matter—is a unity of unmanifest and manifest, emptiness and form. However, if the manifest world is in a constant state of change, transformation, and evolution, that means that a developmental spectrum within the Dharma is necessary in modern times. Emptiness stays the same, changeless, beyond space and time, beyond life and death; however, form evolves over time into ever-increasing complexity and evolutionary fullness. Finally we have the Dharma for our times, empty-free and complex-full at the same time.

What exactly is Spirit in evolution? And, does evolution have an end? In integral spirituality Spirit is both the Ground and the Goal of evolution. It is the Ground or the screen upon which the whole manifests realm appears, including evolution. And it is the Goal of the evolutionary process, a stage-like process of its own fulfillment from matter to Spirit, Spirit-in-Action. At each stage of evolution, Spirit reveals itself like a particular worldspace, a specific perspective. At each stage Spirit speaks to us a certain way. Although evolution is seen as Spirit-in-Action and although Spirit is the ultimate goal of evolution, that doesn't necessary mean that Spirit is the Omega point of evolution.

Rather, spiritual evolution is seen in integral spirituality as a process of endless unfolding.

The key insight of Wilber's integral spirituality is the relationship between state-stages and structure-stages, or better put, their co-dependence. Spiritual experience is always seen, interpreted and embodied via structure of consciousness. There is no spiritual experience independent from its interpretation and embodiment (spiritual intelligence). Here, Wilber is relying on German philosopher Kant who discovered and proved that there is no independent object without an interpreting subject. We don't perceive an object-in-itself, what we perceive is an object plus the structures of knowing of a perceiving subject. Between subject and object there is always a lens through which an object is perceived. In that way, we don't perceive an objective, pre-given reality, we perceive a world which is already a co-creation between subject and object. Goodbye traditional metaphysics and hello co-creative evolutionary age.

What this means for integral spirituality is that both the state-stages (Waking Up) and structure stages (Growing Up) are equally important in spirituality and for spiritual development. Let's assume that two persons are having an intense and heart-opening experience of divine Love during meditation. One person may embody this love like a love towards one's family or nation, another person might extend that love toward all sentient being. The embrace of one's love actually depends on one's structure of consciousness (spiritual intelligence) not on the spiritual experience itself. Or, another example, let's assume that two people see Jesus in their meditations or visions. One person might interpret Jesus as a personal savior and the other person may see an expression of Christ-Consciousness (there is, actually a spectrum of Jesus). Again, the difference is in the lens of perceiving, not in the experience itself. After Kant and especially Wilber, structures of human consciousness simply have to be taken into consideration in spirituality.

Since structure-stages are important as a lens through which spiritual life is interpreted and lived, let us have a closer look to some inherent features for each structure present in today's world. We will use a historical-social developmental spectrum: from traditional to modern to postmodern to integral. It is important to understand that all of those structures co-exist in the present day world. For instance, a church goer is an expression of the traditional historic structure, a business executive abides at the modern level, and an environmentalist at the postmodern one. We will examine those historic structures and the ways they influence the spiritual views and lives of individuals and groups that embody them.

Individuals and groups at the traditional level build their spiritual lives on the strong and puritan distinction between right and wrong. The major spiritual instrument is faith, derived from literal interpretation of sacred texts. The belief in supernatural elements within sacred narratives is common. Individuals at this level feel a strong belonging to the group and approval from the group is crucial. This structure is hierarchical, with very clear roles and identities. Salvation is postponed to after death. Individuals outside the group are seen as simply wrong. The biggest advantage of this stage is a healthy pride in one's faith and group or lineage. The biggest disadvantages are religious extremism that leads to fundamentalism and terrorism.

Individuals and groups at the modern level build their lives on individual freedom and the legacies of science and democracy. The major spiritual instrument is reason, thus the frequent expressions of this stage are deism, atheism and agnosticism. They embrace success and scientifically oriented spiritual practice (experiment, prove, share with others). Advantages of this level are healthy reflexivity and cultivation of reason. Disadvantages are arrogance and aversion towards preceding levels of consciousness, and non-practical and unhealthy skepticism.

Individuals and groups at the postmodern level build their lives based on liberating pluralism. The major spiritual instrument is either relative or holistic reason. Individuals and groups at this level are comfortable with paradox and embrace the Other. It is at this level of historic consciousness that we witness the emergence of genuine religious pluralism. Also, from a spiritual perspective, this level opens a genuine interest in multiple spiritual systems. The advantages of this level of historical consciousness are that it acknowledges the relativity of perspectives and cultivates genuine dialogue and a plurality of perspectives. The disadvantages of this structure are unhealthy relativism, fragmentation, alienation and nihilistic narcissism with its motto "There is no absolute truth, therefore, nobody tells me what to do."

Individuals and groups at the integral level build their lives on integrative holism. The major spiritual instrument is a synthetic, holistic and evolutionary reason. Individuals at this level exercise body, mind, and spirit integration and master various areas and dimensions of their lives. The biggest value of this level of historic consciousness is that it values all preceding levels (unlike the previous levels that declare their own righteousness). Thus, integral consciousness acknowledges that it stands on the shoulders of evolutionary giants and draws its evolutionary power from it. Integral spiritual practitioners are inspired by individual, cultural and cosmic evolution and are true warriors of the transformation of consciousness. It is at the integral level that a genuine unity between life and spiritual practice is possible.

It is important to notice that within one tradition, there are multiple levels of Growing Up. For instance, within Buddhism, there is traditional Buddhism, modern Buddhism, postmodern Buddhism and the new emerging integral Buddhism.

Choose your worldview carefully, my friend. Cultivate and develop it with great love and care. In the present day spiritual world, the right worldview is a necessary ingredient for living a full spiritual life and sharing it with others. The wisdom of the right worldview is very simple: a more comprehensive view is better than a less comprehensive one.

The important consequences of combining the Waking Up and Growing Up teachings are numerous. To start with, let's diagnose the state of spirituality in the present day world. In terms of state-stages, it is clear that Waking Up teachings are unrecognized and not utilized. Throughout Western religious, spiritual and intellectual history, Waking Up teachings (based on a direct experience of Spirit) were suppressed by various religious dogmas and the Age of Reason (western Enlightenment). The consequence of this is that the vast majority of people in our global world do not even know cognitively (not to mention spiritually) that Waking Up growth and spiritual Enlightenment is a possibility for them.

In terms of structure-stages, it is clear that the vast majority of world religions are frozen at the mythic-traditional level. That creates confusion in a lot of people's minds, hearts, and lives, since in other areas—such as home, work, media, hobbies—they abide on modern and post-modern levels. So, in terms of the Waking Up teachings, the world needs to recognize and utilize them. In terms of the Growing Up teachings, religion needs to catch up and open itself to modern and postmodern possibilities. Collective arrested development of religion on the mythic level is one of the most important religious and spiritual issues to improve on this planet.

Utilizing his state-stages and structure-stages teachings, Wilber was able to re-define Enlightenment and to bring it closer to modern-day practitioners. Enlightenment is traditionally defined as Self-Realization, unity of the individual self and Reality, unity of Emptiness and Form. By introducing an evolution component into the Dharma, Wilber now defines enlightenment as "realization of oneness with both the highest state and the highest structure that have evolved at that time in history." In today's world that is nondual state and integral structure. In 2000 BC, for instance, that was causal state and mythic structure. Oddly enough, today one can be equally awake as Buddha but more evolutionary full than Buddha. That is the gift of being born into human condition that is evolutionary wired.

If we connect with straightforward human intuition, it is easy to assume that legendary religious and spiritual founders would today recognize evolution and its legacy and would use it to help awaken others.

Would Buddha go to the doctor? Why not? He would like to stay healthy so that he can teach the Dharma as long as he can.

Would Jesus use Facebook? Why not? Living Spirit finds numerous ways of expression.

Would Lao Tzu value psychology and practice yoga? Why not? It is certainly in accordance with and great supplement to his *Tao Te Ching*.

Here is another illustration of how Waking Up and Growing Up teachings can help us understand spiritual development, spiritual communities and East-West integration. In the 1960's, many spiritual teachers from the East—gurus, yogis, lamas, masters—came to the West to spread the Dharma. Let us not forget that the 60's were, from a spiritual standpoint, about transformation of consciousness. Millions of people were shifting consciousness and introducing new values by experimenting with drugs, music, new forms of political activism, spirituality, lifestyle, etc. In an atmosphere like this, many spiritual teachers from the East felt inspired to bring East-West integration to the next level.

However, the transmission and interaction didn't go without its challenges. On the one hand, eastern teachers appeared to western students enlightened, but not completely. Although at times they were pure, clear and empty; they still showed up as very authoritarian, patriarchal, biased, and, at times, promiscuous, sexist, xenophobic and homophobic. On the other hand, western students were more loose and open on issues regarding sex, drugs, gender roles, politics, culture and lifestyle. Teachers felt free and not that free and students had their share in freedom and openness. This cultural mismatch produced a lot of misunderstandings on both sides and prevented a full East-West integration.

However, if we use the lens of integral spirituality to interpret and understand this confusing situation, it is easy to notice the following: Eastern teachers were very advanced in terms of state-stages (Waking Up) and not that advanced in terms of structure-stages (Growing Up). Western students were fairly advanced in structure stages and not that advanced in terms of state-stages. To be more precise, eastern teachers were at the causal or nondual state-stage and at mythic or rational-modern structure-stage. The vast majority of students were at the gross state-stage and at the pluralistic-postmodern structure-stage. A typical East-West mismatch: East is more advanced in terms of Waking Up and West is more advanced in terms of Growing Up. This is just one example and indication of how integral spirituality can bring East-West integration to the next level and remove misunderstandings and confusion in our global spirituality.

The most important consequence of Wilber's Waking Up and Growing Up teachings is that it brings the integration of Spirit and Life, Emptiness and Form, spiritual practice and everyday life to the next, integral level. Life is evolving, you are evolving, you can engage with myriad dimensions of Reality, all the way up to the final Release into your True

Self and the Original Face. Religion and spirituality are nothing but a conveyor belt of Spirit's own stations. Integral spiritual practitioners are not only involved in spiritual growth but are also co-creating the next level of culture and society. This is where Spirit and Life really meet in our age. We are witnessing for the first time in human history not only a stage-transformation but also a tier-transformation: the integral level of consciousness is the first one to fully acknowledge and embrace (transcend and include) all the previous levels. This $2^{nd}$ tier evolution is bringing to our world evolutionary power, deeper meaning, more inclusion, holism in multiple areas and dimensions, cultural harmony, deeper connectivity and, indeed, higher forms of spirituality. Integral spiritual practitioners contribute to the transformation of consciousness both in terms of Waking Up and Growing up.

One more thing regarding the $2^{nd}$ tier integral structure is of crucial importance for both cultural and spiritual evolution. All the $1^{st}$ tier levels hold that their view is the only one right and show ignorance and aversion towards lower and higher levels within the evolutionary spiral. And this ignorance and aversion doesn't help anyone. Within the integral structure, all the previous levels are welcome—as long as they are healthy and optimal expressions of the values inherent to that structure. For the integral spiritual practitioner, all the stages are seen as stations of life. Although growth is a possibility within every developmental structure, people have an evolutionary right to have a break from growing or to stop growing completely. God bless your station of life, as long as it is healthy and optimal.

This gives us insight on what an enlightened society might look like. It is usually considered that in an enlightened society everyone is equally enlightened and at the same level. However, by acknowledging the evolutionary (station-by-station, level-by-level) fabric of the universe and the human dimension, it is easy to realize that within an enlightened society there would be levels of spiritual consciousness. Everyone starts from square one and develops higher and wider. In that way, traditional, modern, and postmodern levels would still exist in an enlightened society as an evolutionary ladder towards Enlightenment.

Whatever your station in life is—God bless you. Whatever their station in life is—God bless them. The integral lens puts "me" and "you," "us" and "them" in a new relationship and allows more room for cultural harmony and spiritual development.

According to integral research, in Western countries 10% of the population are at the magic level, 40% at the mythic-traditional level, 40-50% at the modern level, 20% at the postmodern level, 5% at the integral level and 1% at the super-integral level (allowing some overlaps). God bless the whole spiral.

# The Way of Wilber

The last crucial thing within integral spirituality is what Wilber calls the 1-2-3 of Spirit. This is another application of Wilber's AQAL (all quadrants, all levels, all states, all lines, all types) model in the field of spirituality. The quadrants are basic perspectives within the manifest realm. Whenever there is manifestation, there is the inside and outside of the individual and collective (thus 4 quadrants). And, consequently, each phenomenon can be viewed via those 4 basic perspectives. Wilber sometimes reduces the 4 quadrants into what he calls the Big Three (I, You-We and It). The 1-2-3 of Spirit is nothing but an application of the Big Three onto the spiritual realm.

Spirit in 3$^{rd}$ person is the objective dimension of Spirit, Spirit as Kosmos (manifest reality from matter to life to mind to soul to spirit, not just cosmos as physical reality), the Great Nest of Life, Great Perfection. The major practice for utilizing Spirit in 3$^{rd}$ person is philosophical and mystical contemplation. By doing it, we observe something objectively larger-than-us which activates and inspires ego-transcendence and spiritual unfolding. From a spiritual standpoint, 3$^{rd}$ person contemplation reveals to us the Ultimate It.

Spirit in 2$^{nd}$ person is the relational dimension of Spirit, Spirit as the Great Thou, our Beloved, our most intimate Friend. This dimension of Spirit is very rich since one can have myriad forms of relationships with the Great Other: one can pray to, be grateful for and devoted to, ask for forgiveness, receive Love, Light and Grace, and much more. The major practices for utilizing Spirit in 2nd person are prayer, kirtan (devotional singing), worship, ritual, forgiveness, acts of service, guru yoga and bhakti yoga. The medium of Spirit in second person is the Heart. When we lovingly connect with someone-bigger-than-us (that is, someone-bigger-than-ego), ego transcendence and spiritual unfolding are almost automatic byproducts. From a spiritual standpoint, 2nd person practices reveal to us the ultimate You-We.

Spirit in 1st person is the subjective dimension of Spirit, Spirit as your True Self beyond birth, death and rebirth, the Seer beyond space-time, the absolute Subject that transcends and includes body-mind-world. To the Spirit in 1st person we awaken to. The major practices for utilizing Spirit in 1st person are formless mediation and self-inquiry. If practiced properly and supplemented with other methods from global spirituality, Spirit as 1st person is the easiest and most effective avenue to Self-Realization and Liberation. From a spiritual standpoint, 1st person practices reveal to us the ultimate I.

We are fortunate and blessed that practices for all 3 faces of Spirit are available to us nowadays. In Spirit X, we strongly recommend utilizing all three perspectives. In the present-day spiritual scene, many spiritual practitioners practice Spirit in 3rd person (Earth-Gaia oriented spirituality) and Spirit in 1st person (mindfulness, meditation, etc).

Due to the negative effects of religion and secularism, we are lacking approaches that utilize Spirit in 2$^{nd}$ person. True devotion can be an important missing piece in the present day spiritual scene: devotion is the best ego-killer (pardon, ego-transcender). When I see and love someone-greater-than-me, I ecstatically open and melt into the deeper dimension of me and Reality. Who is your Beloved, my friend? Who is your Ultimate Friend, the one who has been with you forever, and even beyond?

Have you seen Wilber's vision-logic map with all the quadrants and all the levels? Kosmos with all of its dimensions and all of its evolutionary levels. And the map of your own potential. The map that moves and grows. Awe…

Here is a short guided meditation that can help you taste the states of consciousness.

Close your eyes
Take a few deep breaths
Notice the separate self
And the inherent sense of separation to it
Notice the egoic contraction
And physical and mental aspects of it
Notice the qualities of the gross self and the gross realm
Next, bring your attention to the energetic part of your being

# Spirit X

And feel and realize the world as energy
Notice the boundaries between self and the world softening
Notice the qualities of the subtle world and the subtle realm
Next, surrender and bring your attention to the ever-present void
Deep in your awareness
Feel and realize the causal self and the causal realm.
Next, bring your attention to attention
Or, be aware of awareness
Rest as your True Self
Beyond gross, subtle and causal states and realms.
Finally, relax and let the final boundary between the Seer and the seen dissolve
Simply Be.

With more practice and mastering the states and realms of consciousness, your center of gravity in terms of state-stages will move deeper and deeper all the way to your True Self.

Wake Up, my friend!

Waking Up teachings have been with us for about 50 000 years and Growing Up teachings for only about 100 years, which means that we have less understanding and practices for the Growing Up vector of spiritual development. Here are, however, a few tips on how to grow up.

# The Way of Wilber

The first thing is to be aware that there is something like Growing Up and to familiarize yourself with various developmental maps, such as Wilber's integral model, Gebser's worldview model, Fowler's stages of faith model, Spiral Dynamics, Cook-Greuter self-identity model, Aurobindo's mind model, Maslow's needs model, Metamoderna, Hegelian Dialectics, etc. The good news about these models is that they are psychoactive, it other words, when you digest them cognitively, they start working in your self-system in all possible ways (emotionally, relationally, spiritually, etc.). Being humble when studying the maps is key: remember, the point is not to be at the top stage of the model, the point is to honestly determine where you are in terms of development and to express your stage in a healthy and optimal way. There is always possibility for growth as long as you keep your evolutionary being healthy and are committed to growth. Be humble (in terms of which stage you are at) and be hungry (for more individual and collective growth).

Wilber Growing Up teaching relies on Harvard developmental psychologist Kegan who describes the mechanism of development as "the subject of the one stage becomes the object of the subject of the next stage." Thus, the key for development is to see the self-structure or other structures (relationship, company, history, culture) as an object of development. Clearly, for turning subject into an object some creative distance is necessary. That distance can be inner (meditation, psychological work, education, retreats, embodiment of developmental models) or outer (traveling, living abroad, embodying other cultures, learning foreign languages, retreats and other modes of distancing yourself physically and mentally from daily karma). Embodiment of the model, psychological health, inner and outer distance form self-system and other systems, commitment to growth (individually and collectively) and, indeed, enjoying the process are all guarantees for Growing Up to happen.

Grow Up, my friend!

In terms of three-part structure of the Ways (practice-seeking, Realization, Service-Expression), the Way of Wilber unfolds in the following fashion. The integral spiritual practitioner starts with creating an integral spiritual practice with emphasis on state-training and structure- training. Another thing we recommend here is body-mind-spirit cross-training. Touching all the dimensions of reality (self, culture, nature) is also a key ingredient for this stage. Simply make sure that you are exercising body, mind and spirit and that you are engaging with your self, others (meaningful, soulful exchange) and nature (deep communion). As for Realization, the best is to emphasize state training, structure training, formless meditation and self-inquiry. The Integral model is one of the best containers for Self-Realization since it utilizes the best from East and West and traditional, modern and postmodern legacies. As for Service and Expression, the integrally awakened man and women passionately contribute to the transformation

# The Way of Wilber

of consciousness in various and multiple areas of human existence (self, relationships, work, business, leadership, sports, politics, psychology, technology, spirituality, etc.). Integrally awakened practitioners co-create a more integral and awakened society.

Practices and modules that support the Way of Wilber are meditation, prayer, contemplation, inquiry, body-mind-spirit cross-training, science, technology, relationships, career and many more.

To our evolution and multidimensionality!

# #47
# The Way of the Spiritual Muse

The Way of the Muse is the Way of Liberation and Expression-Service that emphasizes inspiration, release into the Source and the aesthetic-poetic quality of the human existence. In Greek mythology, muses were inspirational goddesses that inspired the arts and sciences. Throughout human evolution, especially in the West, muses were often associated with artists as their source of inspiration. Artistic muses are usually women, although, throughout the history of art, we have some cases of male muses, too. The Spiritual Muse inspires spiritual seekers to release themselves into the Source via her inspiring, radiant Presence.

The Spiritual Muse inspires spiritual unfolding and spiritual Enlightenment as Release into the Source. It is a person, usually a woman, that embodies trans-personal qualities and inspires a trans-personal transformation in the seeker. It is a person that embodies divine qualities and inspires divine transformation and release in the seeker.

# The Way of the Spiritual Muse

O, Muse!
Where are you?
I cannot do this by myself
I need your inspiration.

O, Seeker!
I am always Here with you
Just turn your attention to me.

Ancient poets, writers and historians would invoke divine muses and ask them for inspiration, guidance and creative flow. Many modern artists needed physical presence of muses in order to produce their works of art. Invoking the muse or being inspired by the muse is a deeply spiritual process. One surrenders their being to the Muse and it is, paradoxically, the Muse that does the work. The artist is only the vehicle of the Muse and the Divine. So, at the root of the artistic process involving the inspirational Muse we have a deeply spiritual process of ego-transcendence. Artists always knew very well that real art lies beyond ego and in the divine realms.

O Muse!
I cannot live
Without you
And your Inspiration.

# Spirit X

O Seeker!
I wonder
What is that in me
That inspires you
My braids
My breasts
or
My Presence.

Artistic muses can be seen, at times, as inspirational objects but Spiritual Muses are definitely radiant subjects.

There is a parallel between what a muse is to the artist and what a spiritual teacher is to the disciple. Both artist and disciple project something they already have—and, actually, already are—onto the muse or teacher. However, this inspiring and guiding duality is a necessary part of the process for the vast majority of artists and disciples. A genuine muse or spiritual teacher always points to the Source within when artist or disciple is ready.

O Seeker!
What you are looking for in me
You already have
Constant, effortless Inspiration

# The Way of the Spiritual Muse

The Bliss of Being
Your True Self.

The atmosphere around and within the Muse is poetic and aesthetic. The grass is greener, the sun is brighter, the thought is clearer, the body is more erotic; tastes, smells and sights intensify. Life turns into poetry, a work of art. The Spiritual Muse utilizes this poetic vividness and releases the seeker into the Source. The Spiritual Muse is a movement from the source of inspiration to the Source itself. The major skillful means of the Spiritual Muse is her inspirational, radiant Presence.

O Muse!
Enlighten (me).

Have you seen Cezanne's *Kiss of the Muse* or Dali's *Portrait of Galarina* or Wyeth's *Overflow*? Awe… Artistic muses pointing to something bigger than themselves. Have you seen the larger than life statue of Kuan Yin in the Nelson Atkins Museum of Art in Kansas City? Awe… The Spiritual Muse of Compassion and Enlightenment releasing you into the Source just upon looking at Her.

# Spirit X

Breathe like a Muse.
A simple practice.

Breathe like a Muse, move like a Muse, talk like a Muse, be silent like a Muse, walk like a Muse, sit like a Muse, eat like a Muse, fuck like a Muse, make love like a Muse, inspire others like a Muse and be the ultimate Inspiration… like a Muse.

In terms of three part structure of the ways (practice-seeking, Realization, Service-Expression) the Way of Spiritual Muse unfolds in the following fashion. The Spiritual Muse practitioner centers his or her practice around inspiration and the poetic-aesthetic qualities of life. What is it that inspires you? How does this inspiration feel and where does it take you? What inspires you physically, emotionally, mentally and spiritually? Although the Way of the Spiritual Muse is mostly about human (and divine) inspiration, at this stage it is useful to open to any kind of inspiration such as nature, music, arts, travel and other. As for concrete practices—any opening practices will help at this stage, such as meditation, aesthetic and mystical contemplation, creativity, ecstatic dance and states of flow. When it comes to realization, the key is to move from the source of inspiration to the Source itself ( Inspiration as the Bliss of Being or the Womb of all the universes). Let the inspiration blow

## The Way of the Spiritual Muse

you away into the Source of your being and Reality. Any practice that releases you into the Unmanifested—formless meditation, self-inquiry, silence—is of tremendous help at this stage. Realization for the Spiritual Muse is usually a product of both spontaneous inspiration and the effort of formless practices. Once realization is tasted, mastered and stabilized, the Spiritual Muse is ready to inspire others' gentle release into the Source-Womb-Bliss.

The real juice of the Way of the Spiritual Muse is that it is simultaneously life-for-oneself and life-for-others via the vehicle of human and divine inspiration. No other way puts together the unity of Realization and Expression-Service like the Way of the Spiritual Muse.

We live in times of global crisis, accelerated change and profound transformation. Muses as inspiration for innovative solutions are a necessity in times like ours. If you have any inclinations to this Way, please inspire our evolution and Enlightenment.

The practices and modules that support the Way of the Spiritual Muse are meditation, contemplation, kirtan, movement, dance, silence, relationships, sex, technology, culture and art.

# Spirit X

O, Muse!
Without and Within
Enlighten (me).

## #48
# Ways Are Infinite

Ways are infinite. Spirit is everything and everywhere, so from the standpoint of egoic consciousness, everything is a doorway to Spirit and your True Self. Every moment is an opportunity to awaken to who and what you truly are. And that's the case because at the core of your being you are already That—the biggest paradox and the biggest secret of all.

∞

Spirit X 2.0 touches Infinity and Eternity and unleashes human creativity and divine co-creativity. Spirit X 2.0 is both a teaching and an invitation for co-creation. In that light, follow our Ways and create your own Ways to Liberation that will serve you and others. The Ways are literally infinite.

∞

May you master the Way or Ways to release you into your True Self. May you help others do the same.

Spirit X

# Part IV
# The Book of Codes

# Spirit X

# #49
# CODES AND WAYS

Mastering Ways has become a necessity in times like ours. On the one hand, the manifest world is often too complex and overwhelming for egoic-consciousness, thus touching, resting and stabilizing in the unmanifest dimension of our being and Reality is necessary not only for a spiritual life and Enlightenment but also for living a sane life. On the other hand, spiritual Realization—the royal Way of the Ways and a placeless place of Peace, Bliss and awakened Awareness—is simply not enough any more. You can be very awake and still experience serious problems in your relationship. You can be an enlightened Sage and still have no clue about the economy and practical aspects of your finances. The world of form is complex, rich, and beautiful, and any spiritual teaching in our global and digital times has to bring the relationship of emptiness and form, unmanifest and manifest, to the next level. Form matters and mastering form is a necessary part of spiritual teaching. So with Ways, we glimpse and stabilize Liberation of our True Self and with the Codes we navigate skillfully and meaningfully the relative, manifest reality. The Ways point to our primordial nakedness, the codes give us the subtle clothes we wear and many roles we play in the manifest game of Life. Together, Ways and Codes give us the life of Absolute Freedom, Peace and Fulfillment, the life we all deserve by the virtue of precious human condition.

# #50
# MASTER CODES

Codes are central to the Spirit X teaching, especially its 2.0 version. Codes are various modes of being in relative reality (space-time) and various modes of seeing, understanding and navigating relative reality. As separate selves we are all born into the world and the world can be seen, felt, interpreted and navigated in many ways. The major code you work and live within the human condition—at this point of human evolution—is the code of your relative, separate self. However, the code of your relative self is way more relative than you are aware of. What is your sense of self, right Here, right Now? Are you aware, right Here, right Now, through which lens are you interpreting (and creating, indeed) reality? What is the world for you? Is it a friendly place or not? Does it respond to you, or not? The truth is, my friend, we all don't live in the same world. The world is very different for, say, an environmentalist living in Holland and a housewife living in India. The world can be very different for a democratic supporter and republican supporter both living in the US. And, the world is very different for a 5-year old child and his or her loving parents, living in the same household. With the Codes, we consciously master and embody various ways of being, seeing and living within relative reality.

# Master Codes

Like with the Ways, it is useful to familiarize ourselves with the basic structure of the Codes. Primarily, codes activate and enact the sense of self and the sense of the world. With each code there is a unique sense of self and recognizable and distinct sense of the world; and, of course, to each code there is a specific dynamic—it's duality, after all—between self and the world. Secondarily, Codes activate a sense of connection and a sense of development. Each code creates a unique meaning, interpreting and giving value to the self, others, the world, suffering, Life in general, death, God, etc. In each world-space of a particular Code, the self is able to create various types of connections with other selves, structures, world and the Divine. Also, within certain Codes there is a very clear sense (and energy, indeed) of the development-evolution of the self, other structures and the world. Some codes, also, come with a very clear sense of spiritually, ethics, and aesthetics. And, alas, Codes come and go. We use them skillfully, meaningfully and optimally to navigate the multidimensional relative reality and make it a better place for ourselves and others. Ultimately, we play with the Codes to realize how relative our ego-identification is and how empty, open and radiant we already are.

The convenient thing about the Codes is that they come and can be derived (or borrowed) from myriad areas and dimensions within the human condition. Codes can be personal (Napoleon, John Lennon), spiritual (reincarnation, fierce Grace), historical (Renaissance, 1960's), psychological (Achiever, Player), geographical (Mediterranean, Swiss Alps), cultural (Beat, transcendentalism), pop-cultural (Madonna, Wizard of Oz), political (Martin Luther King, Lenin), artistic (Michelangelo, avant-garde), scientific (Einstein, quantum physics), technological (Steve Jobs, Silicon Valley) or a combination of the above. Codes simply utilize the evolutionary and multidimensional richness of the human dimension. Instead of unconsciously holding onto the sense of lack of egoic consciousness, Spirit X Codes point to and utilize the richness of the trans-egoic dimension of our being and Reality. Implicitly, Codes point to the Empty Host consciousness that we inherently are—which is our ultimate richness, our human-cosmic endowment.

Spirit X 2.0 addresses and reveals the whole of reality in its multidimensional beauty. With the Ways we re-discover our primordial nakedness and openness. With the Codes, we are in a position to create a spiritual-energetic-vibrational closet, with energetic clothes you can wear, selves you can be, worlds you can enact, lenses you can interpret reality with, frequencies you can master, ways you can connect with others and the world, etc. For instance, if you need to build your business, you can activate the Achiever Code, with the Achiever self and the Achiever sense of world which is the field of possibilities for achieving numerous goals or a major goal. Once you have completed building your business, you can gratefully drop the Achiever Code and play with and activate other Codes. If you are going out for the evening, you can activate the Madonna, Queen of Pop Code, have fun, dance and meaningfully sweat with others. If you are interested in spiritual enlightenment, you can activate various Codes (reincarnation, Himalayas) to support you on the Way.

Which Codes are in your spiritual-energetic closet?

The key for activating successfully and playing with the Codes is to see-through egoic-identification, to realize the relative structure of the relative, separate self. If we look closer to our egoic, relative self, it is easy to notice that within it there are other sub-selves or sub-personalities (victim, helper, spoiled child, an American, etc.). It is also easy to notice that within our conventional lives, we all play various—at times complex—roles (father, software engineer, trusted friend, etc.). Codes just bring this richness of our self to the next level. As for the ego—the key is to make it transparent. It comes and goes like many other phenomena in your awareness. Oddly enough, ego can be on board with individual and collective spiritual evolution, by letting the higher dimension shine and get expressed through it. Make your ego an ambassador of Spirit in the human dimension.

# Spirit X

"In the beginning there was the Word and the Word was God" says the opening line of the *Gospel of John*. Yes, indeed, in the beginning there was the Word, a divine creative principle. Codes are echoes of this primordial creative principle, the myriad modes we create-enact and abide in multiple world-spaces.

How to activate Codes? Given the versatile nature of the Codes, there are numerous ways to do that. Let's not forget that Codes, first and foremost, activate a sense of self and a sense of the world. So, if you, for instance, are activating the Achiever Code, you can close your eyes, connect with the Achiever part of you (perseverance, strategy, confidence, etc.), activate that code-vibration within yourself, then open your eyes, look at the world-without and recognize the field of possibilities and friendliness-supportiveness of it, and activate that sense of the world. If you are activating, say, the Mediterranean Code, you can do that with food, traveling, visualizations, or studying. On a good day, all you need to activate the Mediterranean Code is to feel a bit of sunshine on your skin. If you are activating the Madonna, Queen of Pop Code, you can do that by listening to music, dancing, watching videos or having sex. The thing is, the more you open your being via the Ways, the more Codes become available to you. Within your primordial nakedness, there lies an evolutionary and multidimensional field of the Codes. Welcome to the richness of the human dimension.

# Master Codes

Master Codes. Why not? You have already mastered a lot of things. No reason to play small. And what else to do, as we are approaching the Age of Transformation.

# #51
# CHILD CODE

Child Code Go!

Are you getting tired of life and its seriousness and responsibility? Are you energetically drained? Do you feel that, at the bottom of your being, there is innocent freshness that you lost touch with? Do you feel things were better back then, when you were a worry-less child? Well, my friend, you can always activate the Child Code. In the human condition, the child is never lost, it is transcended and included, so you can always reactivate it. Whether you want to improve yourself, your relationship, family, business or the world, the Child code activates extraordinary frequencies and opens a unique perspective.

**Spirit X Child Code**

**Self:** Playful, Curious, Innocent, Growing

**World:** The Field of Play, Wonder and Growth

**Development:** Fast Movement From Childhood to Adulthood

**Spirituality:** Play, Wonder

**Ultimate Game:** Hide and Seek

It's never too late to activate the playfulness within you (self) and to introduce it into various areas of your life (others, world) such as relationship, family, sex, work, purpose, mission and spirituality. Playfulness lightens the self and the world by emanating joyful frequencies. If properly done at the adult stages, playfulness can easily produce the states of ease and flow that can transform many lives and structures. In a world that is becoming heavy, too serious and in desperate need of innovative solutions—the Child Code is the antidote. It is essential to recognize that the child is always within you, it's just a matter of finding his or her appropriate expressions in the adult, mature world.

Feel the boundless energy of the Child Code within you. Use this energy mindfully and skillfully. Yes…

Take few deep breaths, my friend. I want you to see the world through wondering eyes. I want you to see the world as a field of wonder. Every thing infinitely interesting. Every moment radically new and fresh. Your being joyous and open. The world wants to play with you.

Yes, my friend, there is this perspective of the world—all you need to do is to activate it. The truth is, the relative world has infinite perspectives—why not reveal them appropriately.

# Spirit X

Child-self and the world—what a great story and interaction.

Children grow so fast and effortlessly. Growth and development are inherent to their being. And then, we adopt the cultural view that at some point we stop developing. In our both challenging and inspiring times, adult development is key. Yes, my friend, you can grow and develop as an adult; there are numerous stages of adult development. Yes, my friend, you can grow after the age of 28 (the actual age when the majority of humans stop developing); yes, you can grow integrally as a person at the age of 50; yes, you can grow at the age of 70. By activating the Child Code, we remind ourselves of the growth and development, and, indeed, we activate it.

The world wants you to grow.

And then, there is the ultimate game of Hide and Seek. Children love playing it, across ages and across cultures. You hide, remain safe and unseen. You seek, remain open and alert. In a sense, Hide and Seek is the only game there is. Spirit manifesting itself through the act of forgetting itself (involution) and, then stage-by-stage remembering itself and finding its way Home (evolution). By activating the Child Code, we open ourselves to this developmental re-membering and coming back Home all the way to our Divinity.

Activate the Child Code if you want to introduce more playfulness, lightness and energy into your life and the world, cultivate states of wonder, kick-start and enhance adult growth and much more.

Child Code Drop!
You are an Empty Host.

# #52
# WOMAN CODE

Woman Code Go!

Some of us are blessed to be born in the female form (women), some of us are blessed to have some amount of feminine principle and in their self-system (men) and all of us are blessed to experience the feminine energy without, coming from people and the world itself. Although both feminine and masculine principles and energies can have pathological expressions within the human dimension, the goal of the Spirit X teaching is to offer optimal and distilled expressions of the feminine and masculine principles and energies that can be used to navigate relative reality and for spiritual unfolding. As human evolution progresses, we have enough evidence to claim that the future is going to bring about more balance of feminine and masculine principle and energy in each of us and the world. If you are a woman, the Woman Code can help you sharpen your feminine essence. If you are a man, the Woman Code can help you bring some feminine and human qualities into your life and the world, and indeed, understand the feminine better.

## Spirit X Woman Code

**Self:** Open, Embracive, Immanent, Relational, Caring, Compassionate, Birth-Giving, Receptive

**World:** Ocean of Energy, Flow In All Directions, Currents That Connect, Mother, Shakti

**Development:** From Human Feminine to the Divine Feminine

**Spirituality:** Love, Fullness, Embrace, Radiance

**Connection:** Love, Feeling, Touch, Conversation, Healing

**Aesthetics:** Feminine Beauty

---

Close your eyes, my friend. Feel your separate self as open, receptive, full of love, life and energy. Let the life-energy flow through you mind-body. Let Love shine and spontaneously move through your whole being. Connect with parts of your being—physical, mental, spiritual—that have the capacity to give birth to someone or something ( a child, an original thought, a novel, a structure, a spiritual explanation). Now, open your eyes, see and feel the world as currents of energy that give birth, love, nurture and connect. You just activated the Woman Code, in its most pure and optimal form.

# Spirit X

A quick way to activate the Woman Code: praise yourself (no ego inflation, please) and allow others and the world to praise you. Receive the praise. Feel the Radiance, Be that Radiance.

○

Another quick way to activate the Woman Code: make yourself look good. And feel good. The rest is a spontaneous and effortless Radiance of the Woman Code.

○

One more quick way to activate the Woman Code: give birth to someone or something.

○

The world is a fertile field of all possibilities. It receives you fully. It gives you life and energy. It embraces you. At times it gets moody and stormy—but that's Life. Yes, my friend, there is this perspective to the world.

○

Look at the Moon. Look closely, feel fully. Who says the world is not governed by the Feminine.

○

Are you able to be open and receive the world?

Filled in by the world?
Why not?
That's what the Woman Code is about.

If the world makes you dance—so be it.
If the world makes you cry—so be it.
That is the nobility of the Woman Code.

The developmental drive inherent to the Woman Code is a growth from the human feminine to the divine feminine. The egoic feminine self is characterized by a sense of duality between the self and others and the world. With the expansion of Love, Life, Energy, Embrace and Fullness within and without, the sense of boundary between self and the world softens, the feminine self becomes a co-creator with the Divine and , eventually, dissolves—stage-by-stage—into Divine Love-Light. The divine Feminine is the expression of this Love-Light via various means—in this case via the human mind-body.

○

In order to activate and sustain the Woman Code, make sure you nourish the immanent element of the human condition. The Woman Code is all about Immanence and the key is to create practices and situations that nourish feminine Immanence such as feeling Love, Energy and Light

# Spirit X

within your being, taking care of your body, walking barefoot, connecting with your partner and family, connecting with other women, spending time in nature, connecting with the Earth, and caring for the nation, globe and cosmos.

○

Feminine spirituality is ultimately about Love, Fullness and Embrace—in relationships, family and the world. That is the biggest gift of the Feminine in the human dimension.

○

Activate the Woman Code if you need more love, life, and energy in your relationship, family, company, nation and world; if you need to give birth to someone or something (child, poem, song, project or business), if you need to feel more connected with yourself, others, Earth and the world and to bring more care to the world.

○

Woman Code Drop!
You are Naked Awareness.

# #53
# MAN CODE

Man Code Go!

△

Some of us are blessed to be born in the male form (men), some of us are blessed to have some amount of masculine principle in their self-system (women) and all of us are blessed to experience the masculine principle without, coming from people and the world itself. Although both the masculine and feminine principle can have pathological expressions within the human dimension, the goal of the Spirit X teaching is to offer optimal and distilled expressions of the masculine and feminine principles that can be used to navigate relative reality and for spiritual unfolding. As human evolution progresses, we have enough evidence to claim that the future is going to bring about more balance of masculine and feminine principle in each of us and the world. If you are a man, the Man Code can help you sharpen your masculine essence. If you are a woman, the Man Code can help you bring some masculine and human qualities into your life and the world, and, indeed, understand the masculine better.

# Spirit X

△

**Spirit X Man Code**

**Self:** Autonomous, Directional, Purposeful, Missionary, Transcendent

**World:** Directional, Meaningful Whole, Wholes Within Wholes, Challenge, Consciousness, Shiva

**Development:** From Human Masculine to the Divine Masculine

**Spirituality:** Freedom, Release, Consciousness

**Connection:** Reason, Mission, Vision, Challenge

**Aesthetics:** Masculine Beauty

△

The masculine sense of self is characterized by autonomy, directionality, purpose, freedom, consciousness and transcendence. Feel your separate self in all of its autonomy. How is it to be self-determined and a free individual? Identify the goal, focus on it and feel the power of the masculine—and human—directionality. Align with your purpose and allow yourself to be pulled by it. Activate your mind and try to put all of reality into one meaningful whole. Feel the drive for freedom, follow it mindfully and with integrity. Where does this search for freedom ultimately take you? How are others included in that search? Clearly, there are many gifts to the masculine sense of self that both men and women can utilize in navigating reality and on the spiritual journey.

△

What is the masculine sense of the world? Why don't you try it with me, dear reader? Let's put on the lens of the Man Code onto your eyes. 3… 2… 1… The world is moving in purposeful direction and you are part of the movement. The world is a meaningful whole that you can see and understand. Actually, it is whole within wholes within wholes all the way up to Eternity and Infinity. And, indeed, the world can be often challenging. Approach this field of Challenge with courage, perseverance and loving inspired service.

△

A quick way to activate the Man Code: take criticism from a trusted friend or mentor. Notice the appreciation, clarity, energy and the sense of direction, purpose and mission towards greater Consciousness and Freedom.

△

Another quick way to activate the Man Code: challenge yourself—physically, emotionally, mentally or spiritually. How is it to be renewed by being on the edge?

△

Look at the Sun. Look closely, feel fully. Who says that the world is not governed by the Masculine.

# Spirit X

△

Are you called by the world? Do you want to explore it and understand it? Does that inspire you?
Turned on by the world?
Why not?
That's what the Man Code is about.

△

If the world responds and opens to you—so be it.
If the world challenges and tests you—so be it.
That's the nobility of the Man Code.

△

Spine & Heart... Spine & Heart... Spine & Heart. Spine without Heart makes you over-masculine and outdated for our times. Heart without Spine makes you an over-sensitive, postmodern guy, unable to fully respond to the fullness—and at times challenges—of life.

△

The developmental drive inherent to the Man Code is a growth from human masculine to divine masculine. The egoic masculine self is characterized by a sense of duality between the self and others and the world. With the search for more Freedom and Consciousness via release, breakthrough, courage, holistic strategies and spirituality, the sense of the boundary between self and world softens, the masculine self becomes a co-creator with the Divine and, eventually—stage-by-stage—dissolves into the expression of pure Consciousness and Absolute Freedom via various means—in this case via human mind-body.

△

In order to keep the Man Code fresh, make sure you cultivate the transcendent element of the human condition. The Man Code is all about Transcendence and the key is to create practices and situations that cultivate masculine Transcendence, such as spending time in nature, on-the-edge adventures (physical, mental, spiritual), meditation, retreat, creative solitude, bonding with other men and other forms of the masculine, expanding mind and spirit, various forms of emptying yourself out, etc.

△

Masculine spirituality is ultimately about Freedom and Consciousness—in the self and the world. That is the biggest gift of the Masculine in the human dimension.

△

Activate the Man Code if you want more structure, clarity, direction, purpose and mission in your life; if you want to see the bigger picture and build structures, have more perseverance and courage, and bring more consciousness and freedom in your life and the world.

Spirit X

△

Man Code Drop!
You are Naked Awareness.

#54

# WE-THE-PEOPLE CODE

We-the-People Code Go!

Human existence in space-time is characterized by both autonomy and communion. As autonomous beings, we are self-determined individuals in pursuit of happiness and freedom. As communal beings, we come together around shared interests, ideas, values, goals and visions. This coming together is an inherent part of being human and can take many forms such as family, group, team, company, nation, humankind and all sentient being.

"We the People" is the opening phrase of the Preamble to the United States Constitution. The Preamble is a brief introductory statement of the Constitutions' intention, purpose and principles. In Spirit X we use the phrase "We-the-People" to point to inherent human and cosmic bond between humans and to the Code we can use to navigate the world and for spiritual growth and unfolding.

# Spirit X

**Spirit X We-the-People Code**

**Self:** Collective, Unitive

**World:** Field of Possibilities for Us, Mystery, Challenge

**Development:** From We to Sacred We

**Spirituality:** Resonance, Holy Glue, Togetherness, Shared Vision

**Connection:** Resonance, Sharing, Vision

**Ethics:** Honesty, Integrity, Mindfulness

**Aesthetics:** Human Beauty

There is me... and you... and her... and him. We have been brought together by a magic glue and created a deep bond. We resonate with each other. I am defined by my group, my tribe. It gives me identity, meaning, hope, support, energy and vision.

We-the-people self is a collective self, gaining identity, energy and direction from Us.

Of course, where there is Us, there is Them and the dynamics between the two that can take many forms, from conflict, to tension, to creative tension to balance to unity. We live in times when the movement from Us-and-Them to All-Of-Us is happening in many We-Spaces. Such is our global and digital age.

# WE-THE-PEOPLE CODE

What is the glue that connects you with your tribe? Blood, nationality, fashion, clothes, music, arts, tech, politics, spirituality, shared vision, several of these, all of the above? And, what do you do about Them?

Let's take a pause for a while… I invite you to be grateful for all the people you have resonated with in myriad we-spaces. It's great to be human and it's magical to resonate with others. Thanks for reading these words. Thanks for reading this book.

We-the-People, look at the world. Look at that Mystery and Uncertainty. And yet, and yet… feel all the opportunities potentially contained in it, see how it inspires us and supports us, see all we can do together in this magnificent field. If challenges occur, it's only a bump on the road towards our Divinity. Envision what we can do and have together. Envision what our children can have.

Every We-Space comes with its own specific and unique sense of ethics. From a strong sense of right and wrong, to how to see Them, to how to treat insiders and outsiders, to how to unite with Them, every we-space has its own ethics. In Spirit X, we suggest emphasis on honesty (towards the self and the other), integrity, and mindfulness, since those qualities are important both for navigating various We-spaces and for spiritual unfolding (both individual and collective).

We-the-People… We-the-Sentient-Beings… We-the-Cosmos… When we get together, the sky is the limit.

Activate We-the-People Code whenever you want to accomplish something with your group, whether family, team, tribe, company or All-Of-Us.

We-the-People Code drop!
You are primordially Naked.

# #55
# Holistic Code

Holistic Code Go!

Our times are both challenging and inspiring, simultaneously we are facing major crisis in, to name a few, health, environment and economics, and major breakthroughs in, to name a few, technology, science and spirituality. Also, everyday life became complex in both full and overwhelming way. An average global individual handles on daily basis relationship, sex, family, work, finances, health of body and mind, institutional and daily politics, culture and gender worlds, social life, virtual life, purpose, spirituality, and more. On a good day, life appears incredibly full and satisfying. On a bad day, overwhelm is the only feeling and reaction. Good and bad days come and go with us at the mercy of the whole samsaric process.

However, for every level of samsara there is a way out. In complex times like ours, we need models that can hold that complexity and turn it into an advantage of our rich, global life. Luckily, in the past few decades, we are witnessing the emergence, acknowledgment, and embodiment of many holistic and integral discourses. Spirit X Holistic Code makes sure that your ride within the modern global world is smooth, full of ease, flow, meaning and growth.

# Spirit X

**Spirit X Holistic Code**

**Self:** Body, Mind and Spirit Integrated

**World:** Myriad of Perspectives, Evolution from Matter to Life to Mind to Soul to Spirit, Kosmos, Divine Play

**Development:** From Body to Mind to Soul to Spirit

**Spirituality:** Holistic, Integral

**Connection:** Inner and Outer, Developmental

**Aesthetics:** The Beauty of the Whole

The holistic self is balanced, connected and whole. To activate the holistic self simply connect body, mind and spirit and make it a balanced whole. Cultivate a healthy, strong and flexible body via enough sleep, healthy diet and physical exercise. Notice that the right body posture produces the right mind posture (and vice versa). Cultivate body-mind harmony. Follow your thoughts; notice that negative thoughts (for instance, "I am not good enough") feed negative emotions (sadness). Notice that positive thoughts ("Life is good") produce positive emotions (gratitude). Be aware of this dynamic-unity between thoughts and feelings. Master this connection and put it into a balanced whole. Connect with your soul. What soul-task are you working on in this lifetime (in terms of mastering more love and wisdom)? And—hey, why not!—open avenues to rest as your True Self. And, even stabilize that vantage point. Also, as a holistic self, engage fully and meaningfully with at least 3 dimensions of the human condition such as relationship, family, work, sports, business, culture, politics, environment, spirituality, etc. Engaging fully and meaningfully with the world is an inherent part of the holistic self.

The fullness and richness of the holistic self cannot be underestimated. We are fortunate that plenty of practices for body, mind and spirit exist in the present-day transformation industry and that cultivation of the holistic self is a real possibility for many spiritual practitioners. Amen.

Would you like to see the world through the holistic lens? Well, you will need to participate in it: 3... 2... 1... The world is a Divine Play of perspectives. Earth and Sky dance together, nature and culture blend harmoniously in front of your eyes, people come together into higher Unity—and you are a co-creator in that process. Even more and even better—the world is a movement from matter to life to mind to soul to spirit, and, yes, God needs your help in doing this, and, hallelujah, you wholeheartedly turn this responsibility into human-divine play. In the Holistic Code the world is a Stairway to Heaven.

In the holistic perspective cosmos, the physical universe,

becomes Kosmos, evolution from matter to life to mind to soul to spirit. And you are not only an objective, rational observer-manipulator (and at times the victim of circumstances) but a conscious co-creator of this process.

Another gift of the Holistic Code is the sense of connection with others and the world. Not only does the holistic self better understand the world and participates in it in a deeper and co-creative way, but also it establishes deeper connections with fellow humans. The holistic Code truly reveals to us others both externally and internally, and it is this internal seeing of others (who they are individually, psychologically, developmentally, culturally, and spiritually) that creates deeper and more authentic connections between humans. The process can be deepened and extended to all sentient beings.

Development from body to mind to spirit is inherent to the human condition. First we master the body, then we master the mind and, eventually, we master spirit, all in a transcend-and-include fashion. Unfortunately, at this point of human evolution, we are not fully actualizing this inherent potential. The vast majority of people master body to an extent, master mind to an extent, and then get stuck in their further growth as human (and divine) beings. Studies show that the vast majority of adults stop their growth as persons at the age of 28. The reason for this arrested development is twofold: psycho-spiritual growth is not yet fully acknowledged (it is not on our psychological, cultural and institutional maps) and people stop growing as individuals due to the psycho-existential luggage they don't heal and release (trauma, regression, pathologies, etc.). The Holistic Code is here to make sure you continue to grow as an adult too, all the way up to your inherent divinity.

Holistic spirituality includes body, mind and the world into the process of spiritual unfolding and awakening. It is the whole of your being, immersing with the whole of the world, being released into the whole of Reality, and, from there, offering a whole of the Service.

You are a holistic being, Life is a holistic affair: the Holistic Code plain and simple.

Holistic modes of seeing and being are fairly new in our individual and collective consciousness, so it may not be as easy to activate them as some other codes (for instance, the Child Code, which all adults have transcended and can re-include at any point). Thus, as a part of activating the Holistic Code, it may be useful to familiarize yourself with various holistic models.

# Spirit X

We have already mentioned Wilber's Integral Theory in the context of the Ways. Wilber's AQAL model (all quadrants, all levels, all states, all types, all lines) is both a great map of reality as well as a great model for self-development. By honoring the inner, outer, individual and collective dimensions of all phenomena, acknowledging the evolutionary-developmental fabric of the self and the universe, and making room for the spiritual states of consciousness and psychological types and intelligences, Integral Theory can be applied to various areas of our lives (relationship, sex, work) and radically transform many fields and disciplines (business, medicine, spirituality).

Another emerging holistic model is Hanzi Freinacht's Metamodern Politics, which is a new perspective in politics, both coming after and going beyond modern society. The major novelty of this perspective is emphasis on the psychological development of citizens and, as a consequence, Listening Society is a new kind of welfare where emotional needs and psychological growth are a priority. That way, citizens are truly seen and heard (as opposed to manipulated and monitored, which are the major pathologies of modern societies). Just like we noticed in Spirit X, that the starting point of spiritual teachings for the 21st century should be ego-transcendence, Freinacht argues that the political notion of the "individual" has reached its limits and proposes the notion of "dividual" and even "transindividual." With its focus on psychological development, politics and society, as well as understanding of a new emerging creative class and its mission, metamodern politics is a superb model for both our time, characterized by accelerating transformation, and the future.

Activate the Holistic Code for more balance, depth, connection, clarity, love, energy, spirit and wholeness in your life and the world.

Holistic Code Drop!
You are an Empty Host.

# #56
# ACHIEVER CODE

Achiever Code go!

In the modern and global world, we all need to achieve something from time to time and make our life and the lives of others better. Achieving is simply one of the fabrics and perspectives in the global world and, when needed and appropriate, it is important to know how to activate it. Whether you are going through school, getting a degree, building a business or company, playing sports, working on a book or exhibition, improving your health, or seeking spiritual Enlightenment—the Achiever Code is available to help you throughout the process.

**Spirit X Achiever Code**

**Self:** Autonomous, Independent, Progress-Oriented, Strategic, Successful, Educated

**World:** Democratic-Scientific Arena of Opportunity, Progress, Competition and Excellence

**Connection:** Team, Group, Shared Strategy, Shared Goals

**Development:** Progress Towards More Excellence and Independence

**Spirituality:** Growth Through Excellence; Independence; Good Life

Let's activate the Achiever Self. 3... 2... 1... Connect with the perseverance part of you. Connect with the successful part of yourself. You can do this, because you are ready, you have the strategy and you fully understand the game and see through the system. You are growing through the process. You are achieving excellence and that is recognized by others and society. If you need to compete with others —so be it, as long as the rules of the game are clear and fair. If you need to join a team with others—so be it, as long as we share the same strategy and the goals. Winning—in acceptable ways—feels good. Success—under defined rules—feels good. Achieving—mindfully and with integrity—feels good. I am worthy of a good life and am grateful to the world the makes that game possible.

The easiest way to activate the Achiever self: have a plan for your life.

Let's activate the Achiever sense of the world. 3... 2... 1... The world is an arena of opportunities with clear and just rules. It is democratic (everyone gets an opportunity) and scientific (one can build a strategy to win or succeed). The

world opens for you an opportunity to grow through effort, strategy, competition and excellence. The world gives you an opportunity for independence and a good life. If the road gets bumpy—you persevere. If everything goes according to plan—you are grateful.

A quick way to activate the Achiever sense of the self and the world: Recognize the upward mobility texture of the world. Jump on it.

The goal of the Achiever Code both developmentally and spiritually is Freedom as independence and a Good Life to be shared with others (mostly family and friends but often including a wider tribe).

The Achiever Code plain and simple: We all want and deserve a Good Life. And it is achievable through effort, strategy, competition and excellence. Furthermore, others and the world support you in that. What a relief!

Activate the Achiever Code when you need to achieve something, whether short term (going to the gym, losing weight, studying for the exam, improving your relationship) or long term (earning a degree, having a career as an athlete, politician or scientist, writing a novel, making a record, building your business or company, or simply creating your life).

Achiever Code Drop!

You are Empty... And Radiant... And ready to activate another appropriate and optimal Spirit X Code.

Spirit X

## #57
# Player Code

The Player Code Go!

Are you sensing that a lighter way of being is possible, individually and collectively? Are you longing to tap into the creative freedom of Life itself? Do you want to introduce more ease and flow into your daily activities? Luckily, there is the Player Code in the endowment of your human condition.

**Spirit X Player Code**

**Self:** Free, Spontaneous, Creative, Skilled, Immersed, Absorbed

**World:** Lila, Play, Game, Mystery

**Connection:** Togetherness-in-Play, Togetherness-in-Game, One

**Development:** Progress in Skill, Freedom, Connectivity and Absorption

**Spirituality:** Freedom, Spontaneity, Holy Yes!

**Aesthetics:** Creativity, Freedom, Spontaneity, Art

The Player self is light, energetic, playful and creative. It is playful not out of chaos, but out of skill, practice and mastery of Life. Jazz musicians are famous for their creative, playful and spontaneous improvisations, but before they improvise they put years of practice in mastering the skill. Likewise, the Player self is playful not without but through the practice and mastery of various skills or Life itself. The Player knows very well that structure ignites spontaneity and that discipline and practice lead to creative freedom.

"Be Spontaneous!"—we hear that often but it is easier said than done. The truth is, one cannot be spontaneous unless one knows how to release blocks and get unstuck. Although there is the whole art and science of how to release blocks, for the purposes of the Player Code we are going to emphasize a general attitude of non-reactivity to both the inner and outer aspects of Life (acceptance and response rather than reaction to what is) and mastering the skill (something you are good and passionate about) to the point that doing the skill produces a state of absorption and trans-personal spontaneity. Other block-busters include meditation (and other spiritual practices), company and the help of trusted friends, humor, nature and more.

The world within the Player Code appears as Lila, the Divine

# Spirit X

Play in its own spectrum-like fashion. It can be an effortless, goalless, spontaneous display of the Divine, it can be Play with a certain goal, it can be a Game defined by certain rules—nevertheless, the world invites us to play more often than we want to acknowledge. The Player Code applies both to the Play, and to the Game of Life. The Play refers more to a general attitude towards Life and how things are done; the Game refers to a specific activity defined by certain rules, participants and space. The world as Lila invites us to deeply see and relax into the Divine display; the world as a Game of Life invites us to approach life lightly, creatively and playfully; and, specific games of life (sports, education, business, marriage, spirituality, etc.) invite us to honor certain rules, participants and spaces, master our skills and, consequently, improve our characters and the world. The Player Code can be applied to virtually all aspects of our life, from relationship to sex to family to business to culture to politics to environment to spirituality.

The world WANTS you to play? Can you see it?

A quick way to activate the Player Code: Say "Yes!" to everything, internally and externally… Yes! Yes! Yes!

And than—it happens! You are in the Play, or in the Game

and you disappear. You are still in the Play or Game but it's all happening on its own. Your small self dissolves into the Play or Game. You go from being a noun to being a verb. The Player and the Play dissolve into Playing. Just pure Playing. By being fully absorbed in Play, you forget who you are. This holy forgetting opens a deeper dimension of our being and, indeed, doing. This is where the Player Code overlaps with the Way of the Player. And we should say that very few Codes overlap withe the Ways. The truth is, one can transcend mind-body by slowing down the activity of mind and body, or one can transcend mind-body by immersing deeply into the skill and the Play.

"Before enlightenment, chop wood and carry water. After Enlightenment, chop wood and carry water"—this famous Zen saying exactly describes the promise of the Player Code. When we tune in with the Player within us and the world as a Play, we bring together daily life with Luminosity and Depth—and what is revealed to us by doing so is simplicity-within-complexity and lightness-within-depth.

The Player Code is not without its dark side. At its core, life is a Mystery and when we activate the Player Code, we are embracing the unknown. When we step into the unknown we may discover something extraordinary about ourselves and the world, invent something truly original, experience Delight or even Self-Realization; or we may fail and end up disappointed, rejected, sick or even die. With any kind of play we are taking certain risks and, thus, a healthy dosage of risk-taking is recommended at certain stages and in certain moments of the Player Code.

And, of course, there is, then, togetherness-in-Play and togetherness-in-Game. In the Play or Game we share reality, connect as humans on a deeper level and form unique friendships. Whether we re-lax in playing for playing's sake, or transform some areas of life into play, or play a game defined by rules, participants and spaces, whether we win or lose—playing remains one of the best ways to connect genuinely with others.

One of the advantages of the Player Code is that it gives you the "know how," playfulness and confidence within multiple perspectives, dimensions and world-spaces. Once you master a certain Play or Game (say, sports, playing guitar, business or philosophy) you can extend that skill to other activities and perspectives. With the Player Code you can navigate and master sports, business, education, you can lose weight, perfect your body and mind, and have a spiritual awakening. And Indeed, you can help others and transform the world.

# Player Code

Activate the Player Code when you want to lighten and simplify your life and the world in all of its depth, complexity and beauty; to create something that will help you and others; to radically change yourself, others and the world, or simply to play for the sake of playing.

There is no stopping of Lila, within and without.

The ripe skill and free play will save the world.

Yes! Yes! Yes!

The Player Code Drop!
You are an Empty and Luminous Host.

Spirit X

# #58
# Hacker Code

The Hacker Code Go!

We live in a digital age, which means that not only do we use technology on a regular basis, but also that it influences, changes, and transforms everything in our lives, internally and externally, individually and collectively. The digital age influences how we think, feel, behave, connect with each other, how we spend our time, how our society shapes, it informs all aspects of the human dimension. Adjusting and responding creatively (rather than neglecting or reacting) to this digitalization of our lives is becoming an imperative, spiritual practitioners included. In other words, it is better to be a hacker than to be hacked.

By hacker here we don't mean a computer criminal (a person who illegally accesses phone, computer, network or system) but rather a person who is digitally skilled, and culturally and socially informed, and uses creativity to find simple and fast solutions to complex problems. Hacking is a fairly new phenomenon in the human evolution and dimension and it may require mastering certain new evolutionary skills (computers, programming, understanding of the software, etc.)

The Digital Age is a reality and it is here to stay. It is up to us to get familiar with it and to utilize it for noble purposes with the Hacker Code.

### Spirit X Hacker Code

**Self:** Digitally Skilled, Culturally and Socially Informed, Creative, Playful

**World:** Digital, Cultural and Social Complexity; Accelerated Field

**Connection:** Virtual, Mass, Global

**Development:** Simplicity-in-Complexity, Acceleration

**Spirituality:** Flow, Absorption, Inspiration, Virtual Connection

**Aesthetics:** Tech

3... 2... 1... Activate the Hacker Code by familiarizing yourself with your phone, computer and the digital world. For activating the Hacker Code on a higher level, master a certain level of computer programming. Stay socially and culturally informed and get comfortable with the acceleration of the world where good things are getting better, worse things are getting worse and fast things are getting faster. Rather than getting overwhelmed by this situation, get inspired and master the necessary skills to improve your life and the life of others. Use digital solutions to simplify and accelerate your life. Use digital solutions to simplify and accelerate the life of others. Which social and cultural challenges (environment, education, medicine, gender, abuse, whistle-blowing, etc.) are you inspired to improve with your digital skills? Notice and improve your creativity and inspiration. Notice and improve your states of flow and absorption while working on your computer, especially while solving issues you are passionate about. Dissolve the boundary between working and having fun and being playful. Hack...

In a wider sense, hacking is simply a skillful and creative attitude to problem solving and any kind of system. Hack your body, hack your mind, hack the world, hack God, hack consciousness. Of course, in Spirit X we assume that hacking is done mindfully and with integrity.

3... 2... 1... The Hacker Code reveals the world as a digital and multidimensional field of interaction and acceleration. The world has a digital and multidimensional flavor which invites your participation and co-creation. The information is fast and free, the connection is mass and global, various dimensions are dancing with each other. The world invites you to simplify it and to bring the Digital, the Cultural and the Social into a faster, freer and more functional synthesis. The world wants to connect deeper and to grow faster and it needs your help and co-creation. The world and others acknowledge and reward your skill and creativity.

The Hacker Code has an inherent spirituality to it: once we immerse into a digital activity, especially into the creative problem-solving of an issue we care or are passionate about—spiritual states of creativity, flow, playfulness, and absorption are easily available to us. This is possible mostly because hacking is simultaneously work and creative play. The spiritual states available to us in creative digital activities are not to be underestimated since they reveal to us a deeper dimension of our being and reality and can inform literally every other aspect of our lives. Bringing more creativity, flow, and playfulness into our lives, both individually and collectively, is a sure way to radically transform the world.

Activate the Hacker Code to digitalize your life and the life of others, and to find digital solutions (fast, effective and possibly free) to burning cultural and social problems.

Hacker Code Drop!
You are Empty.

# #59
# HIPSTER CODE

Hipster Code Go!

In Spirit X we insist both on the development and enlightenment of spirit and the development and enlightenment of mind. In present day spirituality, cultivating the mind into its synthetic and evolutionary function is an imperative due to the complexity and acceleration of the world of form. Our culture and society require a sophisticated mind to navigate them and that's what the Hipster Code is about.

The history of the hipster phenomenon is rich and ambiguous. From the lifestyle and slang of 1930s black jazz musicians ( who were hip or "in-the-know" about an emerging culture), to the adoption of those values—alongside with racial diversity—by the white middle class youth (as a rebellion to the mainstream culture of the Eisenhower era), to the reemergence of the hipsters in the 1990s and 2000s (embodying new cultural trends and cultural capital in small enclaves in big cities), the hipsters are a constant phenomenon of the global cultural scene. By hipster in Spirit X we mean a person who is informed about the current and emerging trends in culture and society, and who fully lives and embodies those values. The hipster is sophisticated with a deep understanding and embodiment of culture, arts, music, the digital world, environmental issues, etc. In complex and challenging times like ours, we need hipsters, within and without, to help us navigate current trends and create future ones.

## Spirit X Hipster Code

**Self:** Hip, Sophisticated, Fashionably Current, Pulled by the Future, Alternative, Vanguard

**World:** Collage of Cultural and Social Trends and Perspectives, Playlist of Meaningful Songs, Pastishe, Emerging Alternative

**Connection:** Lifestyle, Good Taste

**Development:** From Current to Future, From Alternative to Mainstream

**Spirituality:** Embodiment of Lifestyle and Values, Walk-the-Talk

**Aesthetics:** Hipster

The hipster self is clearly hip, informed by the current trends in the culture and society, often on the margin of culture and society, but nevertheless brings important values and perspectives to culture and society. The most distinctive feature of the hipster self is the fierce, unapologetic, and creative embodiment of new emerging values. The

# Spirit X

hipster self hangs out with other hipster selves creating a strong culture of mutual resonance. To activate and cultivate the hipster self, immerse in culture, music, arts, feminism, environmentalism, digital culture and other fields. The biggest gift of the Hipster Code is its sophistication—the ability to be at Home with and embody many elements of culture and many perspectives.

The hipster points to the new kind of rich—culturally rich. In its without and within forms, the hipster is a reminder that there are other things important in life than money, job, economics and politics. The hipster is culturally rich, he or she has cultural capital that can help all of us. In a cultural and social sense, the hipster is a vanguard to a post-materialist era, expanding the meaning of what it means to be truly rich.

What makes you post-materialistically rich?

Breathe, dress up, read a cool book, listen to your favorite tune, have a great conversation with a like-minded friend, eat healthy food, drink brewery beer, care about minorities and the environment, embody boldly what you stand for, create new values, jump on the cutting-edge of culture—how rich! How hip!

Ready to experience the world within the Hipster Code? 3... 2... 1 ... The world is a collage of styles, fashion, music, arts, new cultural and social trends, new modes of being. The world is a playlist of life-changing, full-of-meaning songs. The world is a field of new emerging values. Most importantly, the world invites you—yes, you, dear Hipster self—to embody this collage-like cutting-edge synthesis. The world connects you with like-minded people in hipster areas. The alternative world embraces and values you. The mainstream world is unsure what to think and do about you. On a quiet night, the world whispers to you just how much it appreciates your boldness in what you stand for.

A quick way to activate the Hipster Code: listen to your favorite song and acknowledge how it radically changed your life. Share it with others and together create a cutting-edge vibration.

Another quick way to activate the Hipster Code: dress up! Let your clothes express your values and lifestyle. Embody your ideas and values in your clothes and attitude. Carry comfortably that cutting-edge vibration.

# Spirit X

With the hipster mode of being there is tension between alternative and mainstream lifestyles and values. The hipster seems to be on the margin of culture and society, representing an alternative lifestyle to the mainstream. But let us not be fooled here. The thing is, throughout human evolution many ideas and values that were on the margin and alternative (scientific worldview and method, democracy, racial equality, jazz music, blue jeans, the grunge band Nirvana and much more) became mainstream and a stepping stones for individual and cultural evolution. That's why we have hipsters and that's the developmental and evolutionary significance of the Hipster Code.

The Hipsters of the world unite!

The spirituality of the Hipster Code is unique, it insists on the embodiment of trends, ideas and values. From clothes to food to music, to the arts to feminism to environmentalism to all things hip—these perspectives are more than obvious in the Hipster's walk-the-talk.

One more quick way to activate the Hipster Code: be Vanguard (in all of its glory and disgrace… and beyond).

Since cultural and social complexity is not going to go away—actually, it is only going to widen and accelerate—it is imperative to sustain the Hipster Code by cultivating the sophistication element of the human condition. Make yourself familiar with the emerging trends in culture and society—some of them may be your saving grace and the way of the future.

Activate the Hipster Code to navigate cultural and social complexity, to feel at Home in the rich world and to create future trends that many will benefit from.

Hipster Code Drop!
You are Unstuck and Free.

Spirit X

# #60
# The 60's Code

The 60's Code Go!

Historically, the 1960's was an era of revolution in culture, society and politics. From a spiritual standpoint, it was a period of expansion of consciousness and liberation in perception, culture, society, politics, lifestyle, pop culture, music, sexuality, drug use and eastern spirituality. Like many other eras and revolutions in human evolution (Ancient Greece, Renaissance, scientific revolution, French, American and Soviet political revolutions, etc.), the 60's are stored—transcended and included—in our collective evolutionary consciousness and can be accessed and re-activated. The expansion of both the self and the world are an inherent quality of the cosmos and the 60's Code is here to help us doing that.

✌

### Spirit X 60's Code

**Self:** Expansive, Free, Revolutionary, Norm-Breaking, Socially Active, Psychedelic, Communal

**World:** Revolution, Expansive and Unitive Field, Growth Towards Greater Freedom, Woodstock, Psychedelic Song, Kaleidoscope

# The 60's Code

**Connection:** Love, Freedom, Counterculture

**Development:** Revolution, Greater Freedom in Self, Culture and Society

**Spirituality:** Expansion of Consciousness, Spectrum of Love, Trip Within and Without

**Aesthetics:** Counterculture, Hippie

Ah, the 60's self... 3... 2... 1... The 60's self is revolutionary and expansive. It relies on outer and inner travel and exploration. It is driven by freedom in the world of form, especially in the areas of perception, culture, society, sexuality, music and spirituality. It expands externally (via social change, politics and science & technology) and internally (via compassionate deeds, drugs and eastern spirituality). Externally, it can land on the Moon; internally, it can land on the True Self. In breaking the boundaries it can be gentle, fierce and at times wild. The 60's self connects with others and the world on a deeper level, creating together nothing less than better world. The 60's self is always with us when we need to radically change the self and the world.

3... 2... 1... See and feel the world as Revolution, as a field that expands towards greater freedom. It looks like a kaleidoscopic, cosmic Unity, it sounds like a boundary-breaking psychedelic song. It whispers to you: "Join the Revolution, it will feel great, it may hurt at times, but you will be expanding and I-the-World will never be the same. You and I are of the same substance and are on the trip to greater Unity and Harmony." Welcome to the 60's sense of the world.

✌

A quick way to activate the 60's Code: get naked with your friends.

✌

Another quick way to activate the 60's Code: listen to Jimi Hendrix.

✌

Every revolution brings with itself a new perception of reality—so did the 60's. A large number of people back then were dissatisfied with the middle class, conformist, materialist, and narrow-minded lifestyle, with racism, unnecessary wars, and non-visionary, corrupted politics; a sense of new harmony and unity among humans emerged in the 60's. From a spiritual standpoint, the 60's are significant since during that time it became clear that the ordinary self lives in a kind of prison-like reality—due to narrow perception—and does not recognize its full potential. In that sense, the 60's unleashed an extraordinary creative power to explore human potential, and to bring about new modes of perception, and, consequently, new modes of living.

# The 60's Code

✌

*Break On Through to the Other Side* sang The Doors whose name was inspired by Huxley's *The Doors of Perception*.

✌

The 60's are usually seen as extraordinary times and revolution in self, culture and society, yet equally important breakthroughs were happening in science and technology. Landing on the Moon is still our biggest act of transcendence-without, transcendence in the outer world. We literally went beyond Earth. Fueled by progress and innovation in science and technology as well as by a fiercely competitive Space Race between the two power houses of the 60's, USA and USSR—an amazing expansion of our physical universe began. From the first sentient being, dog Laika, in space, to the first picture of Earth from space, to the first man, Yuri Gagarin, in space, to the first woman, Valentina Tereshkova in space, to the first close-up images of Mars, to the first man, Neil Armstrong, walking on the Moon —the 60's Space Race provided a series of unprecedented scientific and technological breakthroughs into outer space and transcendence-without beyond Earth. At our core, we humans are voyagers and explorers of the outer and inner universe and the 60's certainly cultivated that important side of being human. The landing on the moon—only in the 60's.

# Spirit X

✌

What humanity needs nowadays more than anything else is transcendence-within, landing on the Inner Moon. Let's all land on the Inner Moon and move our center of spiritual gravity from lack-driven ego to vision-inspired soul.

✌

Look at the Moon—the 60's.

✌

Stanley Kubrick's *2001: A Space Odyssey*—only in the 60's.

✌

The 60's developed a distinct form of spirituality, its three main features being the usage of drugs, interest in Eastern spirituality and new forms of Love. Drugs in the 60's were used for various reasons. Its major spiritual significance is in the radical shift of perception, especially with LSD, and the exploration of the inner world. Although the interest in Eastern spirituality was a bit impatient ("I would rather take LSD that meditate regularly"), immature ("spiritual revolution is quick and it's happening with us") and superficial (emergence of pop-spirituality)—the 60's opened major avenues for East-West integration in the years to come. No 60's, no present-day spirituality—it's that simple.

# The 60's Code

✌

The biggest spiritual contribution of the 60's was the expansion of the notion of Love. Or, even, the vision of Love. In the 60's, Love was a form of rebellion and liberation from the repression of the middle class lifestyle. It was physical and spiritual unity among human beings. It was the emergence of gentleness and nonviolence, a new form of power, indeed—the flower power. And, most importantly, Love was love towards all humans. With the 60's we have an early expression of world-centric Love. Overall, the 60's gave us the the rich spectrum of Love and its expansion to inner and outer universe and its extension to all humans. Unlike the usage of LSD, which is an altered state of consciousness with dangerous health side-effects, or Eastern spirituality, which requires patience that practitioners in the 60's usually didn't have, Love in the 60's was a form of embodied, living spirituality that brought Spirit and Life in the West to a higher level.

✌

How do you embody Love? How big is the concentric circle of your Love?

✌

Activate the 60's Code to revolutionize yourself and the world, to expand self, culture and society, and to connect with others through the 60's spectrum of Love. And, of course, activate the 60's Code to bring back the Spirit of the 60's.

# Spirit X

✌

Inner Moon, here we come!

✌

60's Code Drop!
You are Naked!

# #61
# MEDITERRANEAN CODE

Mediterranean Code Go!

There are places and locations in this world and, indeed, in our Hearts that change our lives forever. We visit them, they blow our bodies, minds and Hearts away, we may visit them again or not, we may be living there later or not—nevertheless, our lives are never the same after being exposed to those places. The Himalayas, Swiss Alps, Mediterranean, Sahara, Grand Canyon, Yellowstone, Paris, Rome, San Francisco have changed the lives of millions of people throughout human evolution. In Spirit X, we bring those places and life-changing experiences to the next level and turn them into Codes that reveal the whole world to us.

There are many reasons why we chose the Mediterranean Code as the first one from this group of Codes. Historically, the Mediterranean is one of the cradles of civilization. Culturally, it is the birth place of many civilizations, cultures and religions (Egypt, Greece, Hebrew, Christianity, Rome, Islam, Byzantine, Ottoman and more). Geographically, it is an area around the Mediterranean Sea, covering Southern Europe, Western Asia, and North Africa with great weather and life conditions. Aesthetically, it is a beautiful place, both naturally and culturally, that has inspired myriad of world-class artists and intellectuals. Today, the Mediterranean is famous for its laid-back healthy lifestyle and is the most visited area in the world.

**Spirit X Mediterranean Code**

**Self:** Relaxed, Culturally and Historically Rich, Evolutionary, Healthy, Balanced, Long-Lived

**World:** Cradle, History-Evolution, Ancient, Crossroad, Beauty, Inspiration

**Connection:** Self, Nature, and Culture in Harmony

**Development:** History-Evolution from the Cradle to Eternity-Infinity

**Spirituality:** Mediterranean Lifestyle, Celebration of Life, Appreciation of Beauty

**Aesthetics:** Beauty in Self, Nature, Culture and History

The Mediterranean self is relaxed, healthy, long-lived and enjoys a simple life. To activate the Mediterranean self, make your own food, make eating with family and friends a pleasurable and meaningful social function, walk wherever you can, live simply without a lot of possessions, spend as much time as you can outdoors, live hands-on and low-tech, cultivate southern warmth (both internally and externally), and bring humor and laughter to every situation. The Mediterranean self has an inherent appreciation of nature, culture, and history since the mixture of the three is its habitat. On a deeper level, the Mediterranean self simply celebrates life. Thus, celebrate life in whatever you do, wherever you are (internally and externally). Ah, the warmth and simplicity of the Mediterranean self.

Have you tasted the Mediterranean sense of the world? Get ready… 3… 2… 1… Here, you are in the cradle of human culture, this is where we settled as We and started our journey towards Eternity-Infinity. Here, you are at the crossroad of nature, culture and history, the crossroad of Europe, Africa and Asia, at the crossroad of the human and Divine. Here, you are in the midst of History-Evolution, layers upon layers of culture and civilization exist simultaneously here, inspiring you to co-create with the Divine further steps for returning Home. Here, you are facing Beauty, both natural and cultural, at every step. Here, you feel the warmth of the South, within and without. Here, you find Inspiration with every breath, every sight, every smell, every bite, every sip of wine, every sunrise, every thunder. Here, you deepen the meaning of life and open your being towards… Eternity-Infinity.

The Mediterranean is one of the cradles of civilization. It is where we settled so that we can grow further. In that respect, the Mediterranean carries within itself the primordial evolutionary-cultural impulse that can be activated, within or without.

# Spirit X

Mediterranean—so ancient, almost timeless. Can you feel it? Can you be it?

A quick way to activate the Mediterranean Code: walk to work.

Another quick way to activate the Mediterranean Code: have a glass of wine with family and friends.

The Mediterranean lifestyle—which can be turned into a form of spirituality—rests upon three basic principles: food/eating, natural movement and socializing. Food and eating in the Mediterranean culture are rather a ritual than a routine within everyday life. It involves making your own food at home, socializing and bonding with family and friends, eating outdoors, lots of humor and much more. The diet itself consists regularly of vegetables, fruits, whole grains, beans, herbs, nuts, spices, olive oil, and occasionally of fish, sea food, yogurt, cheese and wine. The crucial part of the diet is eating with others.

The second, and perhaps most important and original principle of the Mediterranean lifestyle, is the emphasis on natural movement. Although Mediterranean lifestyle does not emphasize physical exercise, it does recognize the importance of taking care of the body and interacting with your environment through regular movement. Natural movement involves manual labor (in the garden and around the house) and especially walking. And, of course, climbing stairs—a place where Mediterranean architecture meets the Mediterranean lifestyle.

The third principle of the Mediterranean lifestyle is a strong emphasis on socializing, both with family and friends. In Mediterranean culture there is an implicit recognition of the health benefits of spending time with our fellows humans. Science supports it by proving that healthy social contacts lower blood pressure, improve the immune system and help us live longer. Health and longevity are the most distinguished characteristics of Mediterranean lifestyle and spirituality.

Take a long walk, my friend, for the sake of taking the walk. Don't think about the destination. Smell, look, relax, let the natural movement activate the contemplative mode. Contemplate nature. Contemplate culture. Contemplate the self. Go up and down the stairs. Upstairs... Downstairs... Sky... Earth... See the Sea.

The Sea is the source of Life. All the major civilizations were built around water. The Sea is Beauty, the Eternal appearing in the manifest realm. The Sea is Vast, the Infinite inviting you to reach to it. The Sea is the Unknown, it's a Mystery, beyond it lie new horizons and possibilities.

Aristotle, one of the Mediterranean intellectual giants, knew it very well: allegedly, he had a habit of walking while lecturing. Even his philosophical school was called Peripatetic School, derived from the Greek word *peripateticos* which means "walking." Take a long walk, Mediterranean-style, my friend.

However, the underlying principle of the Mediterranean lifestyle and spirituality—something common to food/eating, natural movement and socializing, yet transcending and including it —is the celebration of Life.

Eat with family and friends—celebration of Life.
Socialize with the fellow humans—celebration of Life.
Work in your garden—celebration of Life.
Take a walk—celebration of Life.
Bring humor as a response to the challenges of Life—celebration of Life.
Look at the Sea—celebration of Life.
Live healthy and long—celebration of Life.

The Universe provided sunset, Life provided open air, History took care of many layers of cultural beauty, I brought food, You brought wine, we All gathered and celebrated —Mediterranean generosity and its endless cycle of giving and receiving.

Another quick way to activate the Mediterranean Code: get inspired by the world.

If you are a philosopher or a mystic and happen to go to the Mediterranean—without or within—you will understand Platonic and Christian Light.

Activate the Mediterranean Code to introduce more health, longevity, beauty, socializing, culture, history, simplicity, and the celebration of Life in your life, the life of others and the world.

Mediterranean Code Drop!
You are luminously Empty.

Spirit X

#62

# Madonna, Queen of Pop Code

Madonna, Queen of Pop Code Go!

Everybody knows Madonna. She is not only a pop star but also a global cultural icon. In Spirit X, we acknowledge Madonna as the Queen of Pop. Playing with songs, videos, movies, TV, magazine covers, fashion, fame, scandals, boy-toys, sexuality and much more, Madonna created grooves that opened worlds and opportunities for all of us. Her endless capacity to re-invent herself and set new trends perfectly fits the basic Spirit X philosophy about the richness of the human condition and dimension. How many Madonnas are there actually? How many of you are there actually? With how many Codes can you play with?

**Spirit X Madonna Code**

**Self:** Queen of Pop, Dancer, Singer, Liberator, Famous, Smart & Sexy, Re-Inventing, Trend-Setter, Attention-Grabber, Hardworking

**World:** Field of Pop, Stage

# Madonna, Queen of Pop Code

**Development:** Endless Transformations of the Queen of Pop and the Field of Pop

**Connection:** Music, Dancing, Having Fun, Sex

**Spirituality:** Rehearsing, Performing, Pushing the Boundaries, Giving Birth, Making Love to Music and the World, Divine Sweat

**Aesthetics:** Cutting-Edge, Provocative, Sexy, Feminist

**Game:** Smart & Sexy, Liberation

Ready to activate the Madonna, part of you? 3... 2... 1... Madonna sense of self is physically fit, restlessly creative and capable of endlessly re-inventing itself. As such it cruises through many terrains within the human dimension. Its general attitude is provocative and liberating. This self is famous and benefits from both positive and negative attention. It has the capacity to turn scandal into marketing. The Madonna self is the Queen of Pop, of the ever-changing field of entertainment, social, cultural and political content. Being the Queen here means that the Madonna self directly influences the field of Pop, by re-arranging already existing content, creating new values, and when necessary, pushing social, cultural and religious boundaries. Madonna sense of self draws its basic power from physical stamina, liberating movement and creativity. It is sexually active, practicing sex with both men and women in both couple and group settings.

The most distinctive feature of the Madonna self is a fluid

identity based on constant transformation and re-invention. Being this self by definition means endlessly re-inventing yourself and, indeed, endlessly setting new trends within the field of Pop towards more freedom.

See and feel the field of Pop and be the Queen of it. 3... 2... 1... The world is a mass field of entertainment, cultural and social content. Some of it is superficial and some of it significant. You observe and feel the whole field and set new trends within it. The world responds with attention, adoration and respect. The world wants you to be famous and successful. The world is the stage of Pop. Everything within the world is a stage and you are the Queen on the stage. If the misunderstanding between you and the world happens, you are courageous and strong, believing into your trend-setting and liberating mission.

A quick way to activate the Madonna, Queen of Pop Code: dance / express yourself through music / be free.

Another quick way to activate the Madonna Queen of Pop Code: push playfully against cultural or religious authority.

# Madonna, Queen of Pop Code

And, then, there is *Hung Up*, the ultimate pop song and pop video. Everything is there: amazing tune, timeless Abba sample, great dancing, physical discipline Parkour, clubbing climax in the gaming parlor, 47-year-old Madonna in one of her best re-inventions. At 4:23 in the video, Madonna is simulating sex with a large Boombox, music player. The image is beyond Pop: Boombox plays and erects Music and Madonna is on the top. Just like potent Kali-Shakti is on the top of lifeless Shiva-Mahakala, Madonna is on the top of Music. While Shakti makes Shiva alive in the world of manifestation so that he can fully fulfill his mission, Madonna brings Music to the next level. When Pop becomes more than just Pop, we are all in Awe, even if it is provocative and controversial. Only the Queen of Pop can create such an image.

*Like a Prayer* video: brunette Madonna dancing in front of the burning crosses. The sign of our times. What do you do when the crosses are burning?

Just like Madonna cultural icon and her world, Madonna, Queen of Pop Code is ultimately born out of sweat.

# Spirit X

Fanatically rehearsing and practicing—SWEAT.
Dancing and performing—SWEAT.
Sexually active—SWEAT.
Pushing the cultural and religious boundaries—SWEAT.
Giving birth to new creations, values and freedoms—SWEAT.
Not to mention that SWEAT is wet.

Madonna, Queen of Pop Code sense of spirituality revolves around liberation via rehearsing/practicing, performing/dancing and playfully pushing the boundaries. We all know that Madonna is a fanatic when it comes to rehearsing for her shows with her team. Rehearsing is the place where Madonna gains confidence, gets creative and establishes the bond with other members of the show. Also, Madonna knows very well that within the practice there are glimpses of liberation that can be extended to other areas of human existence. The wisdom here is, friends, that rehearsal/practice is the cornerstone of every liberation, creativity, connectivity, confidence, and sense of self. Practice on your own and practice with others and the sky is the limit.

Performing (especially dancing) is another key aspect of Madonna, Queen of Pop Code spirituality. When we perform, we share our gifts with the audience, which for its part—if everything goes well—receives it to heart. Madonna, as a women and a pop-star, fully utilizes spiritual, sexual and performing aspects of dancing, making it one of her most distinctive features and forms of expression. The wisdom here, friends, is: perform and dance whenever you can, there is quite a bit of liberation, expression and creativity there.

The final feature of Madonna, Queen of Pop Code spirituality is liberation through pushing the boundaries. The egoic self and ego-preserving culture certainly can feel repressive and authoritarian at times. One of the Madonna's biggest specialties is to push cultural and religious boundaries in a creative, provocative and courageous fashion. The wisdom here is, friends, if we don't push the boundaries from time to time, we don't grow, progress and evolve (both individually and collectively). And, Madonna is a perfect example of how pushing boundaries does not need to hurt all the time and that, quite the contrary, can be quite a tool for marketing and even self-growth.

The sense of development within the Madonna, Queen of Pop Code is a series of endless transformations and re-inventions of both the self and the world. Although Madonna's career will always be seen as controversial and never-ending, we have enough evidence to conclude that her work progressed towards more maturity and freedom. Madonna's creativity and opus simply matured over time, not to mention myriad groups of people she gave voices to and

# Spirit X

liberated (women, artists, dancers, LGBT, children, etc.). In other words, Madonna, Queen of Pop Code can be used as a stairway to more and more freedom and meaning.

Just like Madonna, the Holy Mother, gave birth to Jesus—and the whole worldspace of Christianity—Madonna, the Queen of Pop gave birth to many grooves and freedoms that have benefited us all.

Madonna, Queen of Pop Code Playlist:
Borderline / Like a Virgin / Holiday / Material Girl / Like a Prayer / Into the Groove / Ray of Light / Justify My Love / Music / Deeper and Deeper / Hung Up

Express yourself, Re-Invent yourself, Be YourSelf.

Have you noticed the ticking clock in the background of the beginning and the middle of the *Hung Up*? Tick-tock, tick-tock, the time is running out, my friend, don't waste your life.

# Madonna, Queen of Pop Code

Madonna, Queen of Pop Code Drop!
You are Naked, Luminous and Self-Manifesting.

# #63
# CODES ARE INFINITE

Codes are infinite. The Codes we chose for this book are the ones appropriate for these times of permanent, multidimensional crisis-evolution, our global and digital age.

Spirit X 2.0 touches Infinity and Eternity and unleashes human creativity and divine co-creativity. Spirit X 2.0 is both a teaching and an invitation for co-creation. In that light, follow our Codes and create your own Codes that will serve you and others. The Codes are literally infinite.

May you master as many Codes you need to be Full, Free, Happy and at Home in the many dimensions of the manifest realm, and to help others be the same.

# #64
# Spirit X 2.0 Reading Completion Congratulations!

**2.0** Congratulations, my friend. Spirit X 2.0 is an advanced version of Spirit X teaching and it may take some time to fully digest it. Spirit X 2.0 is both empty (formless Liberation), and full (navigation and feeling at Home in the world of form), as well as tailored both for our times and the future. It is, also, envisioned to be an open-ended synthesis, which means that it is an invitation for co-creation. We congratulate you on completing the reading and are happy to have you on-board.

Thank you for your Attention. We hope that we have showed your Attention how to get to its Source, as well as how to navigate and feel at Home in myriad corners of all possible universes.

If you have further questions or feel ready to contribute and co-create join us at www.anandamali.com/spiritx.

Hallelujah!

# #65
# COMMERCIALS 2.0

Spirit X: Where Manifest and Unmanifest Meet

Look at the Screen
Empty Screen
Spirit X.

Envision an X in your mind's eye
X is where Infinity and Time Meet
X is a point of creation-manifestation
Which kind of X are you?
Spirit X.

This is Jake. He is a platform engineer at YouReset. He lives in San Francisco. "After work I rush home. I don't do TV and other stuff. All I do is Spirit X. Their latest VR series *Hanging Out With Gods* is amazing. It shifts my perception and reconnects me with myself, others and the world. And, I like reading. Ananda is such an amazing author. Thank you Spirit X, you truly changed my life."

# Commercials 2.0

Music: *Take Me Home, Country Roads* by John Denver…
Let us take you Home: Spirit X.

Music: *Blue* by La Tour. Spirit X: Dharma for Our Time.

We would like to thank to our sponsors without which Spirit X wouldn't be possible: every breath of yours, your wide mind, your open heart, and your Awake Attention.

Spirit X: Keeping Your Attention on You.
Free, Full and Whole You.
Thanks.

SPIRIT X

# Outroduction

# Spirit X

# # 66

# SILENCE

The highest use of language is to point to Silence… and beyond it. You are That.

O

Godhead.

Spirit X

# #67
# WORD

"In the beginning there was the Word."

#68
# Not of This World...

"Not of this world, you must yet be in it."

Spirit X

## #69
# Shiva's Hand Is Raised

Shiva's hand is raised and open: It's all OK.

Ego-identification is fragile, like a drop of water on the leaf of space-time. Any attempt to find peace, happiness and stability by reinforcing it, is a trap. The good news is that there is a deeper dimension of our being and Reality, and even depth beyond depth. You are That.

Whatever is happening with the body-mind-world, you have access to fundamental okayness since that is what you are. Don't forget that. Always start from there.

Tick-tock, tick tock… Can you hear the time running? Don't waste your life. Don't waste our life.

Hush.

# Shiva's Hand Is Raised

What is—right Here, right Now—your note in the cosmic symphony of the transformation of consciousness?

# Spirit X

# Spirit X

www.ingramcontent.com/pod-product-compliance
Lightning Source LLC
Chambersburg PA
CBHW071233290426
44108CB00013B/1391